THE 12 STEPS MYSTICAL HERO'S JOURNEY

2026

READING LIFE BACKWARD FULL CIRCLE

Dr. Christopher Graham, PhD., CCHT

PART OF THE LIFE ESSENTIALS SERIES

THE 12 STEPS of the MYSTICAL HERO'S JOURNEY
READING LIFE BACKWARD FULL CIRCLE 2026
A PART OF THE LIFE ESSENTIALS SERIES

For permission requests, contact:
owhmspub@outlook.com

LIBRARY & ARCHIVES CANADA ISBN: 978-1-997640-66-0

The Ouroboros (Serpent Eating Its Tail)

- Symbol of eternal return, wholeness, and the cyclical nature of life and consciousness.
- In this context, it reflects the "Full Circle" theme of the title—reading life backward, returning to the origin with wisdom.
- It also subtly nods to alchemy and transmutation, which are core themes in mystical transformation.

Moon and Sun

- The Moon represents the unconscious, intuition, and the mystery of inner life.
- The Sun symbolizes clarity, illumination, and awakened consciousness.
- Together, they evoke the alchemical union of opposites—dark and light, inner and outer, masculine and feminine.

Constellations & Geometric Lines

- These abstract astronomical diagrams evoke navigation, guidance, and cosmic order.
- A visual metaphor for "finding your way" through life, with the stars as archetypal signposts.
- They reinforce the idea that the journey is not random—it's mapped in spirit.

Textured, Aged Background

- The parchment-like texture suggests ancient wisdom, secret knowledge, or a manuscript passed down through time.
- This evokes the timelessness of the 12-step mystical path—it's not a new invention, but a rediscovery.

Color Palette (Ochre, Rust, Gold, Deep Brown)

- Earthy and elemental, grounding the mystical themes in something primordial.
- These tones whisper of fire, dust, stars, and spirit—a palette often associated with sacred texts and initiatory rites.

"2026" Centered Inside the Ouroboros

- Positioning the date inside the ouroboros places this moment in time within the eternal cycle.
- Suggests that *now* is your return point, your awakening, your invitation to the journey.

PREFACE
The Journey Within

This revised and expanded edition of Reading Life Backward: Full Circle follows the sacred architecture of the Mystical Hero's Journey—a timeless path found in myth, spiritual transformation, and inner awakening. Each chapter corresponds to a stage in the soul's cycle of forgetting and remembering, of seeking and finding. From the initial whisper of discontent to the profound return to Self, this memoir is more than a recollection—it is a living map. As you turn each page, you walk this spiral with me. In the end, perhaps, you may discover your own full circle.

CHAPTER I
The River Within

This chapter highlights the courage needed to embrace change and the strength found in vulnerability. It reminds us that transformation begins when we step into the unknown with openness and authenticity.

What is the most meaningful thing in your life? It's a question that can sneak up on you in the quietest moments—between breaths, between seasons, between what was and what will be. I once filled pages with answers, offering detailed accounts of where I was and what I was doing, believing those facts somehow made the moment more real. A wise friend gently nudged me to trim the excess. At first, I resisted. But then I realized—some of life's most meaningful moments aren't grand or dramatic. They arrive quietly.

And still, they shape everything.

It is often during the seemingly insignificant moments—the mundane hours, the in-between pauses—that the universe arranges her pieces, preparing us for what's next. The universe never rests. Her rhythms and reasons continue, with or without our awareness, affecting our lives in subtle or seismic ways.

Synchronicity, that whisper of alignment between the outer and inner world, threads itself through both storm and stillness. When we learn to notice, to see truly, we realize that no moment is wasted. Every experience, whether glorious or gritty, is part of the sacred chain reaction we call life. We are, all of us, bound together by it. Whether we acknowledge it or not, the river carries us.

Some people fear this awareness—the shock of consciousness. It's easier to float on the surface than dive into the unknown. But for others, awakening is the most beautiful disruption. Truth, after all, is a gift—sometimes wrapped in discomfort, but always divine.

My own awakening began in the roots of family—through the quiet wisdom of my maternal grandmother, Mary Guthrie Drummond

Plumpton. She wasn't just a grandmother. She was a mother, a wife, a friend, a historian, a museum curator, and an author whose legacy courses through the very veins of my becoming.

She wrote a book called *The Rambling River*, a tapestry of stories chronicling immigration, rural life, and the history of our land: Corbyville, Ontario. The river she wrote of—the Moira—was more than just water. It was life itself. A winding memory. A timeless witness. A path carved not only through the land, but through us.

Inspired by her, I envision the last chapter of my own journey bearing the title *The River Rambles On*—an echo of hers, a continuation rather than a conclusion. Because rivers, like truth, never end. They nourish, they erode, they carry us forward. They are the soft breath of the ALL— the eternal, irrefutable presence that moves beneath everything, the presence I've come to know as the Creator.

We are born of water. We are shaped by it. Without it, we wither. The ALL is the river, the flow, the force that keeps us from drying out inside. It is He who reminds us that we are not drifting alone.

My grandmother's words still hum in my bones:

"The history of any township, originally settled by Loyalists, is really the history of them all... Here in Thurlow, we have another difference – a river – which rambles through our township... It was the first highway of our early settlers... and many times, the source of food. This is a story... which, like our Moira River, rambles through the township, linking time, people and communities."

Time and again, I've returned to that idea of life as a river. Of events as ripples. One action creates the next. One feeling flows into another. We touch each other through the current of experience, whether we mean to or not. When we toss something into that water—an intention, a decision, a truth—it drifts. It echoes. It finds others.

So this book is my ripple. A collection of moments—some divine, some difficult—cast into the river in hopes they'll reach you. Not to teach, but to remind. Not to explain, but to awaken. Because we are all floating in the same sacred stream, and maybe, if we learn to listen closely—to the patterns, the symbols, the soft but persistent pull of synchronicity—we'll remember what we've always known: that we are never alone.

The river is talking. Life is speaking in symbols. And sometimes, just sometimes, your heart already knows what it's saying.

And as life would have it—the more I begin to see the picture, the more questions I have.

Why This Matters

Embracing vulnerability and change encourages personal growth and deeper self-awareness, helping you create a more fulfilling and genuine life.

Reflect on a recent situation where embracing vulnerability led to positive change. What did you learn about yourself through this experience?

CHAPTER II
Anointment in the Mist

This chapter highlights the importance of patience and mindful presence in the face of uncertainty. It demonstrates that patience is not merely passive waiting, but rather active engagement with the present moment.

In 2008, my body began to whisper before I knew I needed to listen. At first, it was subtle—a rumbling sound deep in my chest when I lay down at night. My lungs felt heavy, as if they were quietly filling with something that wasn't air. Still, I wasn't sick—at least, that's what I told myself. But with each inhale, the weight grew. The moment my mind began to drift, my body reminded me it was under siege.

When I awoke the next morning, I felt like I had fallen through the floor of wellness into something darker. I fell hard and fast. What followed was a foggy days of fever, coughing, weakness, and a strange detachment from the ordinary world. Time blurred. Memory dissolved. I entered what I can only describe as a spiritual amnesia. The physical symptoms were sharp; the inner sensations were stranger still.

I had no medical insurance. No safety net. But even if I had, I wouldn't have used it. That wasn't how I was raised. In the country, you didn't go to the doctor unless death had one hand on your shoulder. Even then, you might ride it out with a cup of tea and a prayer. We healed with love and time, not prescriptions.

For three days—or was it five?—I was locked in fever. My lungs burned. I coughed like an old man dying in a dusty house. A visitor upstairs asked my landlord who the old man living below was. I was only forty-six, but in that moment, I was ancient.

I couldn't work. That alone meant something was seriously wrong. I was the type to show up no matter what. But this time, I couldn't move. I couldn't eat. I could barely sip water. I lay in my apartment in the Hollywood Hills, high above Sunset Boulevard, where the skyline of Los Angeles glittered like a distant dream I could no longer reach.

Eventually, I broke down and called Jane, a friend of twenty years. "Could you bring me some oranges?" I croaked. She knew me well enough to recognize the urgency. She came right away.

Nights were long and strange. Around 3 a.m., I would wake and flip through the TV channels—nothing but infomercials and religious programming. Bored, I stumbled onto music channels. That's when I found gospel music. It wasn't something I had sought out—I'd only attended church twice in my life. But the music touched something ancient inside me. It didn't ask me to believe—it simply *was*, and in its presence, I *was*, too.

My apartment was unusual—built into the side of the mountain itself. The bathroom and shower were carved into the rock, raw and beautiful. There was a steam room, unfinished in its design, with cement walls that dripped with healing condensation. I had unknowingly been practicing steam therapy for years, drawn to it instinctively. Heat and water had always been part of my restoration.

I remembered a visit to Montreal in 2003. I had gone to a spa, where I alternated between intense heat and long periods of rest. One evening, while resting after the steam room, something shifted. The noise from the television disappeared. A music I had never heard before—never even imagined—entered me.

It wasn't like Mozart or Tchaikovsky. It wasn't of this world at all. It had no beginning, no end. It was music that *was*. I couldn't describe it then, and I still struggle now. The closest I can come is to say it was like heaven breathing through a harp, timeless and pure. I believe I heard what many call the music of angels.

That experience opened something inside me. But it was only a prelude to what came later.

One night, in the midst of my illness, I decided to take a steam shower. I set up a stereo in the bathroom and played Dido—soft, echoing, cave-like. As the hot water poured down, the room filled with mist, and my body began to unwind. I crossed my arms over my solar plexus, as I often did, instinctively shielding my core.

Then, something happened.

My arms lifted on their own, suspended as though by invisible strings. I stood in a cruciform shape—arms outstretched; body open. I wasn't controlling my movements, but I wasn't afraid. My chest felt like it was being opened—surgically, spiritually, not in pain, but in revelation.

Knowledge flooded in. Not facts, not words—*knowing*. I felt exposed in the best way. I no longer had boundaries. I wasn't floating, but I wasn't grounded either. My feet were irrelevant. I had become a question wrapped in an answer wrapped in a breath.

Then came the understanding:

Do you accept the Spirit of the ALL? Will you be one with Him?

My response was instant. "Yes." Not with hesitation. Not with fear. Just "Yes."

And then—the water changed. The scalding spray transformed into something silky, rich, and sacred. I didn't know the word for it then, but one came into my mind anyway: *Anointment*.

I covered myself in this holy water-oil, letting it touch every part of me, honoring the moment without resistance. I understood I was being consecrated—not by religion, not by doctrine, but by the ALL Himself.

Years later, I would learn about the concept of the *sacred secretion*, and my experience would begin to make more sense. But that night, I didn't need words. I had been called. Marked. Awakened.

This was the moment that changed everything.

It wasn't just an illness. It wasn't just a fever. It was the beginning of my becoming—my anointment into the river of truth, where synchronicity flows and Spirit speaks through signs, silence, and steam.

Why This Matters

Cultivating patience helps you handle life's unpredictability calmly, enhancing your emotional resilience and mental clarity.

Describe an experience where patience significantly changed the outcome. How can you apply mindful patience to current challenges?

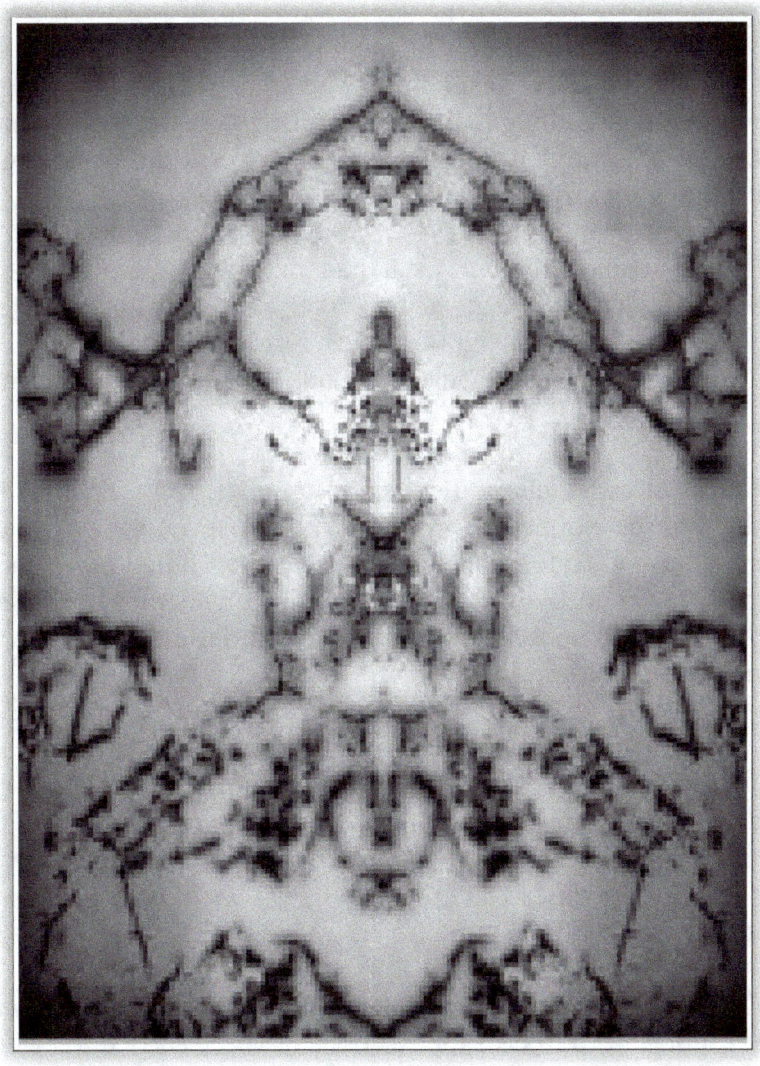

CHAPTER III
Sacred Geometry of Grief

This chapter conveys the importance of recognizing and appreciating life's subtle signs and synchronicities, which often guide us toward more profound truths and meaningful paths.

The morning after my anointment, I woke up entirely healed.

The fever, the coughing, the suffocating pressure in my chest—all gone. As suddenly as it had overtaken me, it had vanished. My body, light and free, felt as though nothing had happened. But something *had* happened. Something profound. A turning. A crossing over. I didn't fully grasp it yet, but I knew I wasn't the same.

As I began piecing together what had unfolded, I realized that my illness—so sudden, so intense—had likely reached its peak between January 10 and January 20, 2008. It was a strange, liminal space in my life, a time when my soul had been made vulnerable without my full awareness.

In the third week of January, I called my mother. A check-in. A hunch. What she told me stopped me cold. My father, seventy-eight years old, had been admitted to the hospital. His heart had failed him again, and this time, he was in a coma. They had him on medication, breathing machines. None of us were surprised; he had defied death before. But this time… something was different.

As my mother spoke, I was silent. Something in me already knew. A shadow crossed my chest like the echo of a final breath. I could feel death drawing near, not just in thought, but in my bones. And for the first time, I wondered: *Was my illness connected to him? Had my body been prepared for this passing in ways my conscious mind could not understand?*

At 9:01 p.m. on January 21, 2008, the phone rang again. It was my mother. I didn't need to hear the words. Her voice carried the weight of them. My father was dead.

The timing struck me with a bitter irony. His death came just three days before my birthday. And, for reasons I may never understand, the family scheduled his funeral on my actual birthday. Maybe it couldn't have waited. Or maybe it could have. Either way, it sealed something in me. That day, once mine, became his. I stopped celebrating birthdays.

Just days after his death, I released a play I'd written a decade earlier: *Perfect Peggy: A Woman's Duty*. It had waited patiently in a drawer, like a story that knew it couldn't be born until something else had died. The play was minimal and raw, set in rural Canada during the 1950s. Through restrained songs and aching silences, Peggy and George—two sweethearts determined not to repeat their parents' mistakes—found themselves trapped in patterns they couldn't escape. A question threaded the entire piece: *What do you do when the right thing goes wrong? Who do you turn to when good intentions become silent betrayals?*

I had poured memories into that script. Memories of my parents' marriage. Of unspoken grief. Of unanswered questions. Now, with my father gone, the story felt more alive than ever.

My siblings reacted to our father's death in different ways. A few shed tears. Some mourned. But for most of us—it was just another day. There were eight of us, six boys and two girls, born in a sequence as chaotic and poetic as our family life itself: girl, boy, boy, boy, girl, boy, boy, boy.

I joked to one of my sisters about the funeral date. "Did you know it's on my birthday?" Without missing a beat, she replied, "Oh, happy birthday!" We both laughed—not because it was funny, but because the truth often is. That moment said everything we needed to say about our father.

We weren't a religious family. My father was Roman Catholic; my mother, Protestant. Some of us were baptized Catholic, others United. I never learned the prayers, never memorized verses, never practiced any rituals. Yet, after his death, something ancient and instinctual rose within me.

I started lighting candles—one each for my seven siblings, one for my mother, and one for myself. I placed a gold coin under each one and let them burn overnight while I slept. I did this night after night, carefully arranging them in symbolic patterns I didn't fully understand at the time.

By the end, I had unknowingly formed a pyramid.

(There is much to be said about pyramids, but that story, too, must wait.)

Meanwhile, I continued my 3 a.m. steam therapy. I listened to more gospel music. I found myself oddly drawn to evangelical programming—not for faith, but for the spectacle. And still, the voice inside me whispered: *There's more.*

One evening, as I stepped out of the shower, something caught my eye.

A line. Faint, barely visible. But something about it pulled at me. I couldn't explain why, but I followed it with my eyes… and slowly, an image began to appear. A face. The profile of a man, carved subtly into the rock of the wall. His nose. His brow. His eyes. His lips. His chin.

The figure was five feet high, nearly three feet wide. Had it always been there? I had lived in that apartment for nearly a year. How could I have missed something so… obvious?

It didn't make sense. I'm someone who notices patterns obsessively— an echo of my Asperger's. But this… this I hadn't seen until *now*. Why now?

There was more, I sensed it. Something hidden just beyond my sight.

A presence. A message. A veil ready to lift. And I knew—my journey had only just begun.

Why This Matters

Awareness of life's synchronicities enhances intuitive guidance, aiding more insightful decision-making and a richer spiritual journey.

Identify a recent synchronicity. How did recognizing it impact your decisions or viewpoint?

the shower wall – close-up later

CHAPTER IV
There's Nothing Here for You

This chapter emphasizes the strength derived from compassion, both for oneself and others. It teaches that compassion is a powerful force for healing and connection.

After my father passed, my brother Mike and his wife, Margot, came to Los Angeles for a vacation with their friends. I was nervous—no, I was *terrified*. This was the first time any of my family would see me in my world, on my turf. And it wasn't just anyone—it was Mike, my oldest brother, my "big" brother. And no matter how old you get, you're always the little one when they're around.

Mike had always been someone I looked up to, admired from a distance. He was a protector—the kind of son and brother who stood guard over the rest of us, especially our mother. A police officer who climbed the ranks with grit and integrity.

My siblings didn't know much about me. I had left home young, and by the time I returned for brief visits, their lives had filled with spouses, careers, kids, and the daily rhythm of parenthood. They had lived through and healed the old family wounds in real time, growing forward together.

I had drifted far away.

My mother served as the nerve center of our family—the filter and funnel of all news, selectively passed along with maternal editing. Through her, I heard about my siblings. But they rarely heard about me.

When Mike and the others left at the end of their visit, something inside me broke loose. A homesickness that had simmered for years finally boiled over. I felt unmoored. I wasn't content. I had the things— apartment, possessions, view—but what I craved most was connection. Family. Belonging.

I had been gone for over twenty-five years.

Once, in a vulnerable moment, I confessed to my family that I wanted to move back home. Their response: *"There's nothing here for you."* I didn't know what to make of that. Did it mean I wasn't part of the "here"? Weren't *they* my family? It left a bruise.

I turned once again to the steam. That sacred, mist-filled space had become my chapel.

During one session, I asked the ALL—the sacred presence that had been slowly revealing itself to me—whether I should return home. I wasn't seeking permission this time—just confirmation. I had spent my entire life going places without asking anyone's opinion. Why start now?

And just then, a vision appeared. Clear as day. A Canadian goose, etched in light right beside the temperature gauge I had stared at a thousand times before. It wasn't subtle. It was a message. *Go.* And so I did. I started packing.

For as long as I can remember, faraway places have called to me. People, cities, cultures—I was always in motion. Some said I was running away. But I always felt like I was running *toward* something. Searching. I didn't know what.

That search nearly cost me everything more than once. There were many moments since 1978 when I was dangerously close to homelessness. But I kept going. I had made a vow at fifteen that on the day I turned sixteen, I was *outta there*. And I was, just like that.

In my final year of high school, I rented a room in town—a jump from a village of 200 to a city of 25,000. And then, in the summer of 1979, two friends invited me west to Calgary, Alberta. I didn't hesitate. I moved back home temporarily to save for the trip, but the ties were already unraveling. That trip marked the true beginning of my journey—and I haven't stopped since.

I've lived in more cities than I can count on two hands. At one point, sitting in a Greyhound station in Phoenix, I started writing them all down to keep track:

Corbyville, ON; Belleville, ON; Calgary, AB; Los Angeles, CA; Belleville, ON; Toronto, ON; Houston, TX; Las Vegas, NV; Palm Springs, CA; Vancouver, BC; Victoria, BC; White Rock, BC; Calgary, AB; Montreal, QC; Quebec City, QC; Ottawa/Hull, ON; Honolulu, HI; Phoenix, AZ; New York City, NY; Burbank, CA—and many returns to the same places in between.

I've moved with only forty dollars in my pocket, no place to stay, and no idea what would come next. And somehow, it always worked out.
I've come to believe that I have a guardian angel. A presence that's protected me, guided me, whispered hard truths, and carried me when I couldn't move on my own. People—often strangers—opened their homes to me. Not always family. Not always friends. But instruments, all the same.

With time, I've realized that many of those people weren't meant to *stay* in my life. They were messengers. Lessons. Just as I've been the same for others. And though they may not remain, the impressions they leave do.

Some believe our lives are prewritten—that our fates and the people we meet are already chosen. I used to resist that idea. But the older I get, the more I see it's not about *control*. It's about *awareness*. Patterns repeat. Signs appear. People come and go exactly as they must.

The road I've taken has been extended, winding, and deeply unconventional. But the road *less traveled* has a voice of its own. A whisper in the dark. A goose on a dial. A line in the shower wall. And somehow, even when I didn't know where I was headed, I was never truly lost.

Because the ALL was always there. Watching. Guiding and preparing me—for something far greater than I could yet understand.

Why This Matters

Practicing compassion fosters stronger relationships, emotional healing, and contributes positively to your mental and emotional health.

Reflect on a moment when compassion changed your interaction with someone significantly. How might you practice more self-compassion moving forward?

CHAPTER V
Goodbye is a Portal

This chapter stresses the transformative power of letting go—of attachments, expectations, and outdated beliefs—to make space for renewal and growth.

Most people find moving on difficult. But should it be?

We cling to people, to places, to things—sometimes even to pain. It's strange how tightly we hold onto what doesn't serve us. There's a saying that the only certainties in life are death and taxes. I beg to differ. The only thing we can truly count on… is change.

And me? I don't mind change. I crave it. I chase it. I live by it. Letting go is my ritual. Change is my confession. And yet, even I—wanderer, minimalist, spiritual nomad—struggle when it comes time to say goodbye. To a home, a job, a relationship. To a self I've outgrown. No matter how many times I've moved on, a part of me still aches as I go.

That ache, to me, is proof of something beautiful: that we are *meant* to feel. That even when we leave, something in us remains. That we were not made by an angry, jealous God, but a loving one who lets us go freely, knowing we may return transformed.

"If you love something, set it free. If it comes back, it's yours." The phrase has many versions, but the truth behind it is universal. I've found that real friendships—real connections—survive time, distance, and evolution.

To make my travels easier, I kept only what mattered. I've lived most of my life with very little money, which meant my choices had to be deliberate. In the end, I always returned to two things: my writings and my photographs. They were the proof of my existence. My legacy in ink and light.

Letting go of my belongings felt, in some ways, like clearing the closet of someone who had passed. Sad, yes. But also freeing. The death of a version of myself. The clearing out for the next.

The day I began packing to return to my hometown, I heard a deafening crash. The sound of shattering glass echoed through the apartment. I froze. Earthquake? No rumble. Just silence.

I ran room to room. Nothing. No broken windows. No fallen dishes. Then I climbed the three steps into the bathroom and saw it—lying on the concrete floor: a photo of my niece Jenny and her husband, Dave.

It had been thrown—*launched*—nearly three feet from the shelf. Alongside it lay a pair of metal X's and O's, decorative but now jarringly symbolic.

As I stood in that strange stillness, something shifted. I looked up—and there it was.

A woman's pregnant belly, unmistakably formed in the wall. The air thickened. The moment became holy. My heart told me what my mind had not yet confirmed: Jenny was pregnant.

I called my mother. We talked casually at first—about the weather, as we always did. Then I asked how Jenny and Dave were doing. My mom, always sunny, always gentle, told me Jenny was heading to the Caribbean with her girlfriends in a few weeks. "Already?" I thought. "A solo vacation so soon after marriage?"

But my mind was elsewhere. I told her about the picture. About the belly. About the crash. I said, "I think Jenny is pregnant." She disagreed. "They just bought a house. They can't afford a baby."
But my intuition screamed louder than her denial. I *knew*.

Still, doubt crept in. Maybe I was wrong. Maybe the crash meant something else—an emotional rupture, a breakup on the horizon. Maybe I had misread the signs.

But I didn't think so.
In the weeks that followed, I went about my move with a quiet calm. I was working hard to find a replacement at Gurney Productions, where I was the Executive in Charge of Production. I boxed up my life, one item

at a time. As I packed my personal papers and backups of photography into a small black box, an eerie thought crossed my mind:

Pandora's box.

That mythic container of suffering and hope. That was my box—holding the weight of my past, the stories I'd lived, the questions I still hadn't answered. It all fit neatly in the trunk of my car.

As strange as it may sound, I had grown attached to that apartment and all its apparitions. I walked the neighborhood one last time, mourning what I had to leave behind.

My convertible barely held a suitcase and two bags. I made one last sweep through the apartment. My chest grew tight. Every wall echoed with memories. Every shadow held a lesson.

Then, one final sign.

Where the photo of Jenny and Dave had once stood—on that shelf I passed every day—there was now the image of a sorrowful face etched into the shelf. A face I had never seen before. The emotion in it was undeniable. I felt it speak: *We're sad to see you go, too.*

I stood in the bathroom one last time, surrounded by my unseen companions. I didn't need to understand it all. I just needed to honor it. I closed the doors gently. Climbed three flights of steps to my car. Fastened the seatbelt. Took a breath.

And drove away.

In a few days I would arrive "home," hoping to find connection. Hoping to finally understand what my family meant when they told me, *"There's nothing here for you."* A phrase that once felt like a rejection would soon become something else entirely.

Because, as I would learn, those words were not cruel.

They were true.

Why This Matters

Learning to let go frees you from emotional burdens, creating room for fresh opportunities and perspectives that enhance your overall well-being.

What is something significant you've recently let go of, and how did it benefit you emotionally or spiritually?

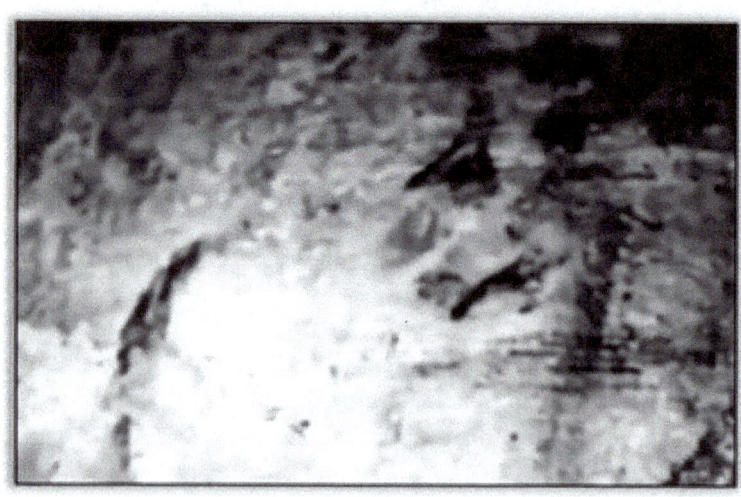

CHAPTER VI
A Room, A Road, A Revelation

This chapter highlights the value of deep listening—to oneself and others—as a gateway to wisdom, understanding, and deeper relationships.

The drive home gave me plenty of time to think—really think.

For decades, I'd brushed off the question: *Why am I so different from my siblings?* But now, with thousands of miles stretched before me, and nothing but time and highway to process it all, I needed answers. This wasn't just about family. It was about identity. About my place in this world.

I've often joked that I'm "the only child of eight." That's how it's felt. While my siblings built lives—steady careers, families, homes—I drifted. Most of them stayed close to our parents, to our hometown. Statistically, half of all North Americans live within fifty miles of their birthplace. I haven't managed to stay in one place for more than a year.

Sometimes, the moves weren't by choice. I once worked as an executive assistant for a well-known Canadian fashion designer. He was high-profile and flamboyant—Peter Nygard. We flew between Toronto, the Bahamas, Los Angeles, and Winnipeg. It was fast, glamorous, intense. Then, one night, while in Los Angeles, something in me screamed: *Get out.* I booked a red-eye back to Toronto and never looked back. Years later, the world learned why. My angels had protected me—again.

But the work I craved wasn't about fashion or flights or fleeting titles. I wanted connection. Deep, soulful connection. But that didn't come easily. For most of my life, I struggled to form long-term personal relationships. It wasn't until much later that I began to understand why—I likely have Asperger's. It explained a lot. My sensitivity. My pattern recognition. My struggle with the unspoken rules of human interaction.

Society loves to reward business success, but I've always questioned that. I met many so-called "successful" people who seemed empty inside. Then there were people like Roger DuBois, whom I met in Montreal. He was warm, authentic, generous with his time and space. He treated me like a friend long before I saw myself as one. We've both aged since those days. Not necessarily wiser—but certainly more seasoned.

I was forty then, bouncing between cities, still searching for my rhythm. Writing about it now, I can't help but laugh. Forty, and still wandering. Should I have stayed in one place? Settled? Maybe. But I've always felt a deep pull to live authentically, even if that meant living in motion.

At one point, I found myself working as a live-in night clerk at a cozy fourteen-room bed and breakfast. The deal was simple: free room, free breakfast, emergency support. In return, I lived minimally, worked part-time, and finally had time to create. During that time, I produced a short film and two documentaries—works now housed in Canada's National Library and Archives. My footprints may be light, but they are real.

With so much unstructured time, I began paying attention. Not just to the world around me, but to the unseen world—the one behind the veil. The spiritual world. My intuition, always whispering, now began to speak louder.

Even as a child, I had *known* things—about people, about situations—things I wasn't supposed to know. That knowing got me in trouble more than once.

While living at the B&B, I developed a habit of walking Saint Catherine Street in the early evenings. Sometimes, I'd wake up with a sense of urgency, like something was pulling me outside. One evening, I stepped onto the street and immediately felt it: the shift.

The air darkened, not in color but in *tone*. The world slowed. Something unseen began to fall over the city like a veil. I slowed my pace—a rare thing for me. In Hawaii, an old man once stepped in front of me and said gently, "Slow down, young man. There's no need to hurry." That memory returned to me now, unbidden.

As I moved through the crowd, the people around me lost their dimensionality. They flattened. Shadows of themselves. Cardboard cutouts with hollow smiles and stiff limbs. It was as if I had stepped into a black-and-white dream while the rest of the world continued in color.

I went home shaken but not frightened. I had seen something. Felt something. The next day, I called my mother. Her voice trembled.

"Auntie Margaret passed away," she said. I cried. Deep, from the gut.

And suddenly, the experience from the night before made sense. It echoed another moment years earlier when her husband—my Uncle Steve—had died. That same shadow. That same slow-walk dreamscape. The thinning of the veil.

I couldn't deny it anymore. I *feel* death. I *sense* it before it comes. Not as a horror, but as a passage. As a truth.

Why This Matters

Practicing deep listening strengthens your emotional intelligence, improving both personal and professional relationships and enhancing your intuitive skills.

Recall a situation where deep listening helped resolve a misunderstanding or offered clarity. How can you implement deeper listening practices in daily interactions?

CHAPTER VII
No Permission Required

This chapter illuminates the courage necessary to follow your own path despite external pressures and societal expectations.

At birth, I was named William David Graham. But everyone called me Billy. *Billy Graham.*

Yes—*that* Billy Graham: Reverend Billy Graham. You can imagine the teasing. Kids can be cruel—adults, too, in their own condescending way. I didn't choose the name, but it followed me everywhere like a billboard I never asked to wear. And never in a million years did I imagine I'd one day be writing about it—let alone invoking the name willingly and AND becoming a Reverend. Ahhh, life. I suppose that's its humor.

I was the sixth of eight children—six boys, two girls. We used to chant our names like a roll call:

Debbie, Michael, Johnny, Jimmy, Mary Ellen, Billy, Gordon, Steven.

It was a competition—how fast could you say them in order? Our own family version of a nursery rhyme, full of pride and identity.

But years passed. Seasons shifted. And now, I was returning "home" not as Billy, but as Christopher.

To some, I may have felt like the lost Graham sibling—an apparition of a brother. "Who is this… Christopher?" I wondered how they'd explain me to their friends. *A brother? Where has he been?* In small towns, if it isn't seen or heard, it doesn't exist. I had vanished long enough to become a legend.

Then came the reintroductions. Meeting nieces and nephews in their twenties for the first time—people whose baby photos I'd never seen, whose birthdays I'd never celebrated. Strange and wonderful.

Bittersweet. And in every moment, I reminded myself: *There's a silver lining, if you're open to seeing it.*

My father wasn't around to meet Christopher. That was a blessing.

He had been abusive—emotionally, physically, and spiritually—alcohol, prescription pills, violence. The humiliation still echoed. I had spent much of my waking life hating him, if I'm open. And even now, it's a complicated grief to navigate. But one thing was clear: I could return home without his shadow.

At twenty-seven, I was emotionally immature for my age. Several psychics and Tarot readers told me so. "You're living in a cloud," they'd say. Maybe they were right. I had always dreamed of a beautiful life. I just hadn't found it yet.

But I held onto one vow I'd made to myself as a teen: *Never punish the future for the crimes of the past.* Don't hold new people accountable for the old wounds. It's more complicated than it sounds. But I don't — even now.

"My father chose my name, and my ancestors gave me my last name. That's enough—I choose my way."

Soon enough, I was on the move again—this time in search of peace, privacy, and silence. I wanted to be away from the noise, the televisions, the comings and goings of strangers.

Just me… and the sound of my own name.

Why This Matters

Staying true to your authentic path fosters more profound happiness and fulfillment, aligning your life with your core values and dreams.

Reflect on a recent decision where you honored your authenticity over external expectations. What did this teach you about your inner strength?

Chapter VIII
Bloodlines & Breadcrumbs

This chapter emphasizes the transformative power of gratitude, highlighting how it shifts perception and enhances the meaning and joy of life.

The homecoming… that wasn't.

It wasn't a celebration. It wasn't a return to open arms. It wasn't the emotional reunion I'd romanticized over twenty-five years. What it was—at best—was a slow confirmation of something I had suspected all along: *There really was nothing here for me.*

Some people leave home young and remain tethered only by memory. Time dulls the edges. The pain softens into forgetfulness. Meanwhile, those who stay reconcile family wounds through shared experience—holidays, births, deaths. But when you've been gone for decades, time moves differently. You show up, and everyone has moved on. You're not missing. You're just… *the other*.

I had also wondered: would the supernatural still follow me here? Were the strange experiences I'd had in Hollywood Hills bound to that land, or were they the echo of something inside me—something reaching for belonging?

One afternoon, I sat in the living room with my mother and a nephew she had helped raise. We swapped stories, fragments of family memory, when Jenny and Dave walked in—yes, *that* Jenny and Dave. The ones from the flying picture and the pregnant belly vision. As they joined us, I felt a magnetic pull toward Jenny. She had that quiet look—one that says, *I've got something to share.*

My mother finished her story, and right on cue, Jenny lit up: "Well, I've got some news."

Before she said it, I *knew*. Beaming, she announced she was pregnant.

My mother's joy radiated through the room. There was always room for another baby in our family of many. Jenny told the story of her doctor visit, how they'd waited until they were sure to tell anyone. I sat there half-listening, my mind replaying the scene in my Hollywood Hills apartment—the picture flung from the shelf, the image of the belly on the wall, the timing of it all.

I asked her how far along she was. Seven weeks. I did the math. I had left L.A. on June 18th. The vision happened days before. I chuckled. "Well," I said, "I believe I know *exactly* when Dave's sperm met Jenny's egg." Laughter broke the room, but I wasn't joking. The signs were real. And accurate.

They laughed too—amused, polite, but skeptical. They're too secular to believe in prophecy, especially from a wandering relative they barely knew. But for me, it was another confirmation that Spirit speaks—if we're willing to listen.

Still, despite the joy of that afternoon, I knew in my gut I wouldn't stay. I had whispered dreams about "coming home" for years. But sometimes, we romanticize what we've never had, thinking we can find closure in a place that never knew us fully. As it turns out, closure isn't something you find. It's something you *realize*.

So I drifted in the meantime—spending time with my sister and her husband, soaking in the quiet and the space between.

Then came another encounter—another I'll never forget.

On a hot afternoon, I sat with my brother John in the living room. Out of nowhere, he shared something that had haunted him for years: when he was nineteen, he had struck and killed an elderly man while driving a heavy construction truck.

It was an accident. A tragic one. I remembered whispers of it from childhood but never knew the details. That day, John told me he'd always been uneasy about the court outcome. Our grandfather Ralph had attended the hearing sitting silently in the back. John believed their shared connection to the Freemasons—Ralph and the judge—had somehow influenced the verdict.

But the next day, at a local golf course, the universe unveiled another piece of the puzzle. I joined my sister and her husband for a post-game beer—a sacred Canadian tradition. At the table sat an older gentleman named Jim Koresh. He radiated kindness. We connected instantly.

Jim had been the Minister of Transportation for the federal government. He knew my grandfather, Ralph, well. And then, out of nowhere, he told *his* story.

He had worked with Ralph when Ralph was just nineteen, delivering liquor from the Corby Distillery. Jim was younger. One day, a man stepped in front of their truck and was struck and killed. Ralph had been devastated. The town grieved. And life, eventually, moved on. But as Jim spoke, something clicked.

My grandfather had never spoken of that moment. But decades later, when *his* grandson faced the same trauma at the same age—nineteen— he showed up. Quietly. As presence. As understanding. As unspoken support. I was stunned.

Why had my brother shared *his* story the day before? Why had Jim told *this* story, after years of knowing my sister, only now, to *me*? These aren't coincidences. They are threads. Messages. Confirmations.

When I shared the story with my mother, she gasped. She had never heard that story about her father. But she understood it immediately. *The unspoken acts of love always mean more than the words.* Especially in our family, where "I love you" was rarely spoken—but often lived.

Later, when I told John—privately, gently—he brushed it off. "Nah," he said. Disbelief. Dismissal. He was married to his conspiracy theory. As most people are. The truth didn't matter as much as the story he'd told himself all these years.

And that's when I realized something fundamental: *just because you are family doesn't mean you are alike.*

I had been used as a messenger—again. As always. And as often happens, my message fell on deaf ears. But that didn't make it any less sacred.

The universe speaks in flashes. In fragments. In milliseconds of meaning. If you miss the signal, the message dies—and history repeats itself. But if you catch it, if you really catch it, something shifts. The past becomes part of the present. The pattern dissolves.

As a child, I remember my grandfather once telling me, *"No matter where your travels take you, the roads will always lead home."*

I used to think he meant that physically—like returning to a house, a town, a place. But now I understand: *He meant something else entirely.*

Why This Matters

Practicing gratitude regularly enhances emotional resilience, positivity, and deepens your appreciation for life's simple joys.

List three things you're deeply grateful for right now. Reflect on how acknowledging these enriches your daily experience.

CHAPTER IX
Ten Dollars and a Wristband

This chapter reveals the significance of embracing uncertainty as a powerful opportunity for innovation, creativity, and personal breakthroughs.

If you've never taken a long solo road trip in silence, I highly recommend it. It's more than travel—it's therapy. Soul work. You come face to face with your thoughts, your patterns, and whatever you've been avoiding. Just… do your research. Bring water. A spare tire. A backup plan. Because if you're anything like me, you'll dive in headfirst with a half-charged phone and a prayer.

Looking back, it's only by the grace of the ALL—my guardian angels, spirit guides, Christ Consciousness, and the Holy Spirit—that I've made it through so many of my wanderings relatively unscathed.

One summer in 2005, I drove from Littleton, Colorado, to Hollywood, California. According to Wiki Answers, it's about a 14-hour journey. I made it in eleven. No food. Three or four Red Bulls. And one miraculous detour I'll never forget.

There's not much between Colorado and California but asphalt and heat. Hours of highway stretch without a gas station or sign of life. If you break down, you're on your own. And if you're not prepared, well… you're SOL.

But once I get something in my head, I act. I had to get to L.A. That was it. So I hopped into an old Honda Civic I'd bought off a friend and hit the road.

A few hours outside of Las Vegas, I spotted something up ahead—just a dot at first. Maybe intuition, maybe vision. But something told me it was a person.

As I got closer, my instincts kicked in. A figure walked alone in the scorching desert heat. I eased off the gas. No one should be out here. Not like that. Not without shade. Not with nothing for miles.

My foot found the brake. The Civic coasted to a full stop a quarter mile ahead. I checked the rearview. The figure just kept walking. Calm. Steady. I backed up.

He was young, maybe late twenties, Hispanic, holding a near-empty bottle of dirty water. His clothes were dusty, skin weathered, soul weary. I looked into his eyes. Not threatening. Not panicked. Just… tired.

"Want a ride?" I asked.

We were both unsure—two strangers aware of the risk. But he nodded, and I opened the door. Truthfully, he didn't have a choice. Had I not stopped, the desert might have taken him.

The first stretch of road was quiet. He reclined the seat and slept. I studied him as he rested. He hadn't bathed in days. He looked dehydrated, maybe hours or even minutes from collapse. But there was something gentle in his spirit. Something intact, even after everything.

About an hour in, he stirred, sat up slowly, looked around, and asked where we were. I told him we were on the way to Vegas.

I handed him a fresh bottle of water. He drank it like someone who didn't know how thirsty they'd been.

Eventually, he spoke. He was from Santa Barbara. Divorced. Two kids. No work. One day, overwhelmed by life, he boarded a freight train heading—he thought—south toward Mexico. He needed to disappear. Think. Escape.

But the train went northeast toward Denver. Two days in, an employee found him and kicked him out in the middle of nowhere.

He hadn't eaten and had no money. Just wandered until he found the road.

Then I found him. We said little. I've found that sometimes silence builds more trust than questions.

As we neared Las Vegas, I was running on fumes—physical, emotional, spiritual. And quite openly, the odor in the car was making me nauseous.

So I booked a cheap motel with two beds. I paid. I didn't want him to feel like a charity case. I didn't have much, but I had enough for this.

He washed his clothes in the motel laundry while I showered. Then he showered while his clothes dried. It wasn't even noon. We rested for a few hours, and by afternoon, we were back on the road.

As we approached L.A., I asked where he wanted to be dropped. He didn't know. He had no money. No plan. Deja-vu for me. He thought maybe the Pacific Coast Highway—he'd walk north toward Santa Barbara and hope for another ride.

I couldn't do that to him. I'd been *him* before—sitting in a Phoenix bus station, alone, broke, hoping for mercy.

I remembered I had an unused return ticket from L.A. to Palm Springs. We drove to the downtown Hollywood bus station and asked if it could be exchanged for a one-way ticket to Santa Barbara. It could. Relief washed over both of us.

As we waited for his departure, I reached into my pocket and handed him ten dollars—my last ten. I didn't mention that. I never do. It's not about the amount. It's about the moment. It's about grace.

He was stunned. Speechless. Then, with trembling hands, he took off a yellow rubber wristband and gave it to me.

"I don't have anything else," he said. "But I want you to have this… as a thank you." It was priceless. I wore that band for almost a year.

Then we shook hands, and I watched him disappear into the bus station crowd. I never saw him again.

Why This Matters

Welcoming uncertainty promotes growth, flexibility, and innovation, equipping you to navigate life's unpredictability with confidence and creativity.

Identify a recent uncertainty you're facing. How might viewing it as an opportunity change your approach?

Faith, Hope, Love

CHAPTER X
The Silent Collapse

This chapter underscores the importance of interconnectedness and collective wisdom, reinforcing that growth is amplified when shared with others.

My answers weren't in Corbyville.

They weren't hidden in the fields where I grew up or buried in the family stories I'd longed to reconcile. Within days of returning, I knew: the romantic idea of *home* was a mirage. The people, the land, the past—it had all moved on, and so had I.

So I packed again. And headed for New York.

When I left, my mother cried. She'd never done that before. Maybe that should've comforted me. Instead, it confused me. *Why now?* Was it guilt? Was it love? Or was it simply that she knew something I didn't? I was empty—spiritually, financially, emotionally. But I pressed on. Because that's what I do. I go. I move. I search.

But the deeper I searched, the less I found.

I sought out answers from society's "authorities"—churches, universities, helplines. But they had none. Or worse, they had no response at all. No echo. No acknowledgment. Just... *silence*. And sometimes silence is louder than rejection.

New York was never a dream of mine. It was just the only direction left.

I had no job, no winter clothes, no plan. Just a place to crash—thanks to Jane. She'd become a kind of surrogate sister to me over the years. Her door was open, and for that, I am forever grateful.

I arrived, still wearing optimism like a loose cloak. I thought maybe— just maybe—this could be a fresh start.

But within days, the world collapsed.

The Great Recession of 2008 hit like a tidal wave. Millions of people lost their homes, their jobs, their savings—their sense of security. Futures evaporated like smoke. I watched it happen in real time. The line between survival and collapse was razor-thin.

And I was on the wrong side of it.

Unemployed. Isolated. Hiding in an unfamiliar and no way forward. The loneliness was deafening. The despair, suffocating.

There were nights I wouldn't have made it through if not for guilt. Guilt that someone would have to clean up after me. That Jane might discover my body. That my mother would have to bury a child. That was the thin string keeping me tethered to life.

I never wanted to hurt myself. But the pain of realizing that *everything* I believed in—dreams, meaning, the system—might be a lie? That almost killed me.

So many people I've known have ended their own lives. When I think about their final moments, my throat tightens, and tears press against my eyes. What did they feel in that last second? Relief? Fear? I pray they found peace.

By fall, I still had no job, no food, no prospects—and no boots. No winter coat. I had spent most of my life on the West Coast where "cold" meant you needed a hoodie. Now, I was in a place where cold could kill you.

I needed a lifeline.

Enter Daryl.

We'd met in 2004 and kept in touch ever since. He was thirty-five years older than me, part-father, part-uncle, part-sage. Daryl wasn't just a friend. He was family. He saw me—the whole of me—and didn't flinch. He was intuitive, spiritual, and had lived through more American history than most textbooks.

He knew, without me saying it, that I was in trouble. One day, with certainty in his voice, he said: *"Get in your car. Drive back to Palm Springs. Now."*

He didn't have much, but I always had a place at his home—even if it meant sleeping on the porch. In Palm Springs, during the summer, that was a blessing.

So I drove. Another long road with barely enough gas, money, or hope. But it was better than sitting still and dying slowly in a city that had no use for me.

That drive showed me two things: First, that this continent is breathtaking—majestic, sacred, and tragically underappreciated.

And second, that the economic collapse of 2008 was more dire than most will ever admit. In town after town, I passed gas stations with empty pumps. That's right—dry. No fuel. A country on the edge, pretending everything was fine.

By the grace of the ALL, I made it.

Scarred. Shaken. But whole. Back in the desert, surrounded by mountains and silence, I tried to rest. But peace was elusive.

I had spent years photographing my journey, documenting my path— not for fame, but for proof that I *was here*. That I mattered. That there was meaning in my wandering.

One day, I opened my files. Gone. All of it.

Years of high-resolution photos—memories, moments, sacred signs—vanished. The only remnants were the low-res images I'd uploaded to a website. It felt like losing a limb.

And then, my last possession of material value—my sports car from Hawaii—was repossessed.

In less than a year, I had lost almost everything.

Almost.

Because even in the wreckage, there was breath. There was awareness. There was *me*.

What do you do when you're standing in the ruins of everything you've built? When you don't know where you're going, and you barely remember where you've been?

You breathe. You cry. You pray. You wait for the next whisper from the ALL.

And then… You start walking.

Why This Matters

Recognizing and nurturing interconnectedness fosters supportive communities, collective healing, and shared prosperity, benefiting both individual and collective growth.

Reflect on a recent experience where collaboration or shared wisdom profoundly impacted you. How can you nurture greater interconnectedness in your life?

CHAPTER XI
The Echo of Loneliness

This chapter emphasizes the profound truth that inner peace and self-awareness cannot be achieved by simply changing environments—true contentment arises from within.

In 2006, once again, the itch returned. The kind of boredom that goes deeper than restlessness—a soul-level ache for meaning, connection, *something*. I was tired of pretense. Of performance. Of cities obsessed with fame and fortune. I didn't want to be near a celebrity, money, or those driven by either. I needed spirit. And silence.

So I returned to Hawaii.

I took a job in an industrial section of Honolulu, working for a company that made glass cubes for walls and showers. Not glamorous, but it paid the rent. My coworkers were few—a recovering alcoholic who talked constantly about her recovery, her friends' recoveries, and a trio of warehouse guys who acted like they were auditioning for the role of "Most Macho."

It was quiet work in a noisy part of town.

One afternoon, just days into the job, I heard shouting outside the garage bay door. At first, I ignored it—just another loud exchange in the neighborhood, I figured. But something didn't feel right. I stood, walked to the entrance, and saw all three warehouse guys standing still, watching.

A man—disheveled, angry, wild-eyed—was manhandling a woman. They looked like they lived on the streets. She clutched a roll of copper, and he squeezed her wrist. She pulled one way, he yanked the other.
She was maybe thirty-eight but looked older, worn down by life. He was a jagged tomcat of a man—half-chewed ears, old scars, animal aggression. As I watched, he ripped one of her earrings straight from her ear. And the warehouse guys did nothing.

I stepped in. No plan. No thinking. Just instinct. I grabbed his wrist mid-strike. "This isn't between you and me, man," he said, eyes flaring.

"It is now," I replied. "You're on private property. What you do off it is your business. But right now, it's mine." He backed down. She walked off, copper in hand. He followed, still muttering.

I returned to my desk shaken. Not so much by the violence, but by the stillness of those around me. Silence is sometimes the loudest form of complicity.

A few minutes later, the store manager approached. "Don't ever do that again," she said. "It's dangerous. Around here, they live by their own rules." I understood. Her concern came from a good place. But I grew up with violence. I knew its silence. I knew its shadow. And I knew this about myself: *If I can make a difference, I will. I cannot bear witness and do nothing.*

The next day, I saw a job listing in the local paper. Comptroller. Restaurant. Downtown Honolulu. I called, interviewed, and was hired by the end of the week. I quit the glass cube job immediately.

The restaurant was *Indigo*, nestled off a city park in the heart of Honolulu. Connected to the Hawaii Theatre, it was lively, elegant, chaotic, and beautiful. The owners, Glenn Chu and Dave Stewart, were the best employers I've ever had—gracious, grounded, real.

The job had layers—HR, accounting, operations. Bar, restaurant, live music, everything under the sun. And I made it run smoothly. In just a few weeks, I needed to be there only a few hours a day.

At first, I thought the job would help me meet people. Make friends. But human resources doesn't lend itself to intimacy. You can't be "one of them." You have to remain neutral, steady, untouchable. And while I liked almost everyone, I stayed apart.

One day, I forgot my keys. Instead of going home, I sat on the restaurant's steps and waited for someone to open up. As I sat there, I noticed something strange—something *dark*. I was silently cursing every car that passed. My thoughts were ugly. Harsh. Condemning. I caught myself.

Where was all this coming from? I didn't know those people. They hadn't done anything to me. But I was seething at strangers.
That night, I went home unsettled.

As always, I parked, rode the elevator to the main lobby, checked my mail. The concierge was there, as he always was. Silent. No greeting. No acknowledgment. Just a cold, blank face.

I walked to my unit and sat in silence.

Loneliness had seeped into my bones. I hadn't noticed how heavy it had become until that day. It wasn't the job. Or the people. Or even Hawaii. It was me. My rhythm never seemed to sync with anyone else's. Not in any city I'd lived.

And the truth was clear as the Pacific sky: *No matter where I go… there I is.*

Why This Matters

Recognizing the source of your personal unrest or contentment as internal empowers you to create meaningful, lasting changes in your life and fosters authentic connections.

Reflect on a moment when changing external circumstances did not resolve your inner feelings. What did this reveal about your internal journey and personal growth?

CHAPTER XII
Magic Island, Sacred Night

This chapter illustrates the mysterious and sacred nature of divine timing and intervention. It reminds us that even in moments of frustration and disillusionment, grace can appear in unexpected forms—and that our small choices can become part of a much larger spiritual orchestration.

It began like any other evening in Waikiki. I left my condo and walked toward Magic Island, a ritual I'd developed to soothe my spirit. That rocky peninsula within Ala Moana Beach Park became a sanctuary of sorts—seventy-six acres of water, sky, and breath between the artificial and the eternal. There, I'd sit in stillness and watch the sunset fall into the sea, the waves pounding the shoreline like an ancient lullaby.

But that night, the world felt... off.

Construction lights blazed like false daylight, illuminating the chaotic intersection near the Ala Moana Hotel and shopping center. The noise was deafening—drills, engines, honking horns. Tourists wandered aimlessly, caught in a vortex of confusion, and cars surged through yellow lights like the rules didn't apply.

I thought to myself: *This is the perfect setup for tragedy.*

It matched my mood—frustrated, cynical, unmoored. I crossed the intersection, angry at the world, angry at its negligence, angry at everything. I reached the park and tried to settle my mind. I sat by the water, stared into the darkening horizon, and breathed.

By 9 p.m., the park began to empty. I turned back.

Still mentally chewing on everything wrong with society, I approached the same intersection—and that's when I saw it: a plastic bag tumbling across the sidewalk. It floated like it was underwater, caught in a slow-motion breeze. I knew I should pick it up. Normally, I would. But tonight, in silent protest, I decided to let it pass.

Let the world clean its own mess.

But the bag didn't pass.

It hit my foot and stopped.

I stared at it. Defeated by the moment, I bent down and picked it up.

That's when I saw her.

A tiny elderly woman stood ahead, pushing a cart overflowing with plastic bags. Of Asian descent, no taller than four foot ten, she moved slowly, almost imperceptibly. I asked if the bag was hers. She said yes. I tucked it back in her cart.

It should have ended there. But it didn't.

As I waited to cross the street, something told me to turn back.

Don't ask why. Just turn.

I did.

The woman's cart was stuck on the curb, threatening to tip her into the street. I rushed back and steadied it. She thanked me softly. Her voice was warm but distant, as if her words were being spoken through water.

I asked where she was going. She said the Ala Moana Hotel.

She was headed in the wrong direction.

Apparently, she and her daughter had been shopping earlier in the day. Around 2 p.m., her daughter left for another errand and told her to return to the hotel on her own—presumably by the skywalk. But here she was, nearly seven hours later, still lost.

My heart sank.

I looked at the hotel in the distance. Lights glowed on the upper levels. Valets stood idle. Bellhops chatted in clusters. And this woman—this *mother*, this *someone's grandmother*—had been wandering for hours through a concrete maze, invisible to the world.

We made our way to the base of a long, steep staircase leading to the hotel. I asked if she thought she could climb it. She said yes.

So I hoisted her cart.

It was heavy. Ridiculously heavy. How she had managed it, I'll never understand. Halfway up, there was a landing. We paused. She caught her breath. Then we continued.

At the top, the hotel revealed itself—a gleaming palace of marble and fountains, of light and spectacle. We crossed the massive driveway and entered the lobby.

I asked if she recognized it.

She hesitated. Then nodded. "Yes."

I started to say goodbye, but she reached for her purse, insisting she would pay me. I gently took her hand to stop her.

It was the softest, warmest hand I've ever held. She did not need to "tip" me.

I walked toward the bell captain's desk to ask for help.

When I turned back…

She was gone.

Nowhere.

Not in the lobby. Not near the elevators. Not behind any pillars. The cart, the woman—vanished.

I blinked. Scanned the space again.

No way.

Just minutes earlier, I had been right beside her. I hadn't been gone more than thirty seconds. It was impossible.

I was still reeling when I remembered the flight attendant I had seen earlier, sitting near the fountain, about to light a cigarette. Surely, she would've seen us. How could she not?

I approached and asked. She had seen us. Thank the ALL.

I told her what had happened—how the woman disappeared. The flight attendant, curious now too, offered to return with me to the bell captain and verify my story.

We entered together, and she gave her account. As she spoke, my eyes drifted to a young Hawaiian bellhop standing across the lobby.

He looked at me. Smiled. Nodded
.
Then gave me the Hawaiian "shaka" hand gesture.

It was subtle—but something passed between us. A knowing. Like he *knew* what had happened wasn't ordinary. It was *meant*.

The flight attendant and I left together. She said something simple as we parted:

"You did a good deed."

It shouldn't have hit as hard as it did. I've done good deeds before. But that moment—her voice—made it feel sacred. Like the entire evening had been orchestrated by something greater. A test. A message. A reminder that even in darkness, we are being guided.

And the night wasn't done.

I walked into my building, expecting the usual silence from the concierge. But this time, he looked up, smiled, and struck up a warm conversation. *How was your evening? What a lovely night, huh?*

I was stunned.

Then my phone rang.

The voice on the line was muffled, almost otherworldly. The man said he owned a historic house in Waikiki and had just gotten my message about a tour guide position I'd applied for a month earlier. The house was supposedly haunted. At the time, I thought it might be a fun side gig.

I'd forgotten all about it.

But this man—this *voice*—had somehow reached me at my new number. A Los Angeles number. One I hadn't given out. One I hadn't forwarded.

When I asked how he got the number, he didn't answer. Just kept talking, as if none of it was strange.

I told him I was moving back to the mainland and wouldn't be able to accept. He was polite. We said our goodbyes.

And I stood there, phone in hand, heart racing, mind spinning.
A plastic bag.
An old woman.
A disappearing figure.
A flight attendant.
A mysterious call.
A concierge who suddenly *sees* me.
A bellhop who seems to know.
A "good deed" that wasn't just a good deed.

It was too much to be coincidence. Too layered. Too seamless.

That night, as I lay in bed, I wondered—had I just entertained an angel unaware?

Had I been called, not by phone, but by fate?

Whatever it was, I knew this much:

I had been seen. Chosen. Touched. Reminded.

Why This Matters

Understanding that we are often being guided—even when we don't recognize it in the moment—fosters faith, humility, and an openness to mystery. Trusting that the universe is conspiring for our growth invites us to act with compassion, presence, and courage, especially when we least feel like it.

Recall a moment in your life when an unexpected encounter or event seemed too meaningful to be coincidence. What message or transformation did it bring? How might you remain open to divine intervention in everyday life?

CHAPTER XIII
Return, Remember, Reveal

This chapter reveals the layered and multidimensional nature of spiritual awakening. Through cycles of returning, photography, light phenomena, and intuitive resonance, it shows that the universe speaks through symbols, synchronicities, and sacred echoes of the past.

In 2004, I landed in Palm Springs via Phoenix, thanks to the charity and kindness of Joe Ordway. I had met Joe and his good friend, John Paul Davis, during a vibrant visit to Montreal—a time when my creative instincts were firing.

But as all things do, that moment passed. I was broke. Joe stepped in, a friend in the truest sense, offering me refuge in Phoenix with no expectations—just friendship. And that was all I had to give.

Not long after, I found myself once again in Palm Springs, my life replaying in déjà vu. Another bus ride. Another long stretch of empty reflection. A suitcase in one hand, barely a dollar in my pocket, and the guidance of the ALL whispering over my shoulder. I walked down the street toward the bar where a longtime friend, Paul Danos, worked.

Paul and I go back to the mid-80s, to West Hollywood, where we had once been roommates. He was one of the funniest people I've ever known—big-hearted, charismatic, sharp-witted. A lovable rascal who knew how to play the game of life. When I showed up, Paul welcomed me without question and gave me a temporary home in his spare room.

On New Year's Eve, 2004, I found myself at the bar where Paul worked, snapping photographs for a local magazine I freelanced with. I had no money, no supplies, but I was hungry for something creative. The flash of a camera was all I had to ignite something in the dark.

After the countdown and cheers had faded, I walked home through the quiet Palm Springs streets, where the night gardens and glowing palms were like luminous poems written by unseen hands. I snapped pictures along the way, drawn to shadows and silhouettes, intrigued by shapes carved by moonlight and man.

As I paused in front of one particular house to photograph a tree aglow with soft lighting, I felt a chill down my spine. My eyes locked on a house down the street—something about it made my heart stutter. That visceral moment, familiar and unsettling, made me turn more than once to check if I was being followed. But there was no one. Just the hush of the desert and something—something unseen—watching.

That was the night I had my first *tangible* paranormal experience.

My landlord, Daryl James, had always been generous and respectful. He let me use his computer and offered me his camera in exchange for photographing local events for the magazine he sold ads for. Though I never thought photography would become anything more than a pastime, it was through his camera that my eyes began to open to the invisible.

One photograph changed everything.

While reviewing images from that New Year's Eve, I came across one of a beautifully lit palm tree. In the background, framed faintly but distinctly in light, were four outlined figures—like the statues of Easter Island—serene and still, like guardians. I returned to that spot again and again, trying to recreate the shot. Same time. Same angle. Same camera. But the figures never appeared again.

I told myself it was nothing. I buried the moment, let the busy demands of life dull its edge. But my subconscious refused to let it die.

A few years later, I found myself once again in Palm Springs. The cycle repeated, but something was different this time—I started seeing patterns. My intuition, now seasoned, recognized signs I had ignored before.

I had never gotten the photo of the half-man, half-monkey face on the mountain. I couldn't draw it if I tried. But when I saw that same face appear again—this time on the bathroom wall of my new home—I knew. It was the same face. The same presence. I recognized it instantly, even though I hadn't captured it with a camera.

During that time, I was working at a small resort hotel. At thirty-three years old, having once brushed against the edges of professional success, I was now making beds, folding laundry, and cleaning toilets. But I worked like it was the most important job on Earth. That's a principle that's both shaped and punished me—this internal drive to do everything well, to see dignity in the seemingly undignified.

Palm Springs was in bloom that year—the wettest season in recorded history. The desert exploded with color. I had never seen anything like it. Walking became my meditation. The camera, my third eye.

And then something else happened. Something… otherworldly.

I started noticing lights. One in particular—on the side of a nearby hotel—would flicker when I passed. Not always. Not randomly. Only when I approached. It would flicker violently… then stop once I passed. I started testing it, approaching from a block away, slowing my walk, trying to surprise it. But the pattern held. It was responsive. It knew me.

Then, I began noticing streetlights—how they would dim or go out as I walked beneath them, only to return once I passed. I started counting them. Noting them. Different streets. Different nights. Different cities.

Always the same experience.

I dismissed it—until one night, stopped at a traffic light in my car, I thought to myself, *Would the streetlights still react to me if I were driving?* Just as the thought passed through me, the light overhead went out.

I froze. Hair on end. Skin electric. The air charged with something unexplainable. The ALL was near. Watching. Guiding.

That was the night I knew the lights were not just coincidences. That I wasn't just walking through the world, but the world was walking with me. Speaking in symbols. Flickers. Faces in mountains. Guardians in photographs.

Triangulation is the act of measuring by connecting three points forming a truth. Phoenix. Palm Springs. Montreal. The past, the present, the future. I didn't know it then, but I was mapping my soul across time, guided by intuition, revelation, and flickering light.

And I was only beginning to understand how far I had come—and how much further there was to go.

Why This Matters

Recognizing patterns in your journey invites deeper trust in your intuitive senses and spiritual experiences. It reinforces that your life is not random but a carefully drawn map—one that rewards attention, reverence, and openness to the unseen.

Have you ever experienced a repeating sign, symbol, or location that felt charged with spiritual meaning? What message might it be revealing to you now? How might you "triangulate" your past, present, and future to find deeper direction?

CHAPTER XIV
High above Sunset, Far beyond Earth

This chapter explores the concept of callings—not as loud declarations, but as gentle, strange, and mystical nudges from the universe. It reveals how even the seemingly absurd or coincidental moments may carry deeper meaning, calling us toward a larger truth about who we are and where we're headed.

My life was getting more bizarre by the minute. Watching the night sky is probably mankind's oldest form of entertainment—silent, slow, but spellbinding if you're patient. One particularly strange evening in April 2008, I stood on the landing outside my Los Angeles apartment, gazing over the city skyline when I saw something flying that didn't quite belong. A UFO? I couldn't say for sure.

Instinctively, I rushed to grab my camera and began videotaping. By now, after so many mystical happenings, I was used to having a recording device nearby. If something supernatural was going to appear, I wanted proof. I also dialed my mother, as I often did during strange moments—it helped to have a witness, even if only on the other end of the phone line.

The object drifted off into the night, and I hurried inside to download the footage. My heart pounded with anticipation, hoping I had caught something remarkable. But when I played it back, it turned out to be a blimp—yes, a blimp, lit up like a Vegas showgirl. I laughed aloud and shared the joke with my mother. It was still exhilarating.

But then something even stranger happened.

As I stood on the landing, laughing to myself, a sudden glow caught my eye. I turned to look at the cement retaining wall of the house below— a blank, twenty-foot slab of concrete that wrapped up into the driveway. And there it was: the word WELCOME, glowing brightly across the wall in massive, unmistakable letters.

WELCOME? Who was being welcomed? My first thought flew back to the blimp—was there something else I hadn't seen? My pulse quickened. Yet as the adrenaline settled, I tried to make sense of it. Where was the projection coming from? The winding roads of the Hills made it unlikely that light could be aimed so directly. I saw no light source, no cars pulling in, no party—nothing.

The next morning, I walked down the hill to inspect the wall in daylight. No sign of equipment. No lights. No projectors. Nothing.

It reminded me of a peculiar night years earlier in Honolulu's Chinatown. During a bustling First Friday art walk, my friends and I visited the Louis Pohl Gallery. A fortune teller there had people draw two stones from a small container. I pulled a red star and a white stone. She looked at me, eyes wide. "You're an alien," she said softly. "Did you know that?"

My friends laughed, but I blushed. She continued. "There are a few of you here, not many, but you're not alone. And they're coming back for you—in five years."

That was 2007. I was 45. She was saying I'd be gone by 50. That date, 2012, stuck with me.

Later that night, I returned home to my high-rise Waikiki apartment and looked out over the city skyline. My eyes landed on a revolving restaurant atop a nearby hotel, glowing in neon. In the moment, it looked just like a spaceship. I'd never noticed it before. Coincidence? Maybe. But maybe not.

Now, back in L.A., standing outside that night, the word WELCOME on that wall felt connected somehow. To the blimp. To the prediction. To all the apparitions and signs that had been piling up like breadcrumbs. My life seemed to unfold in coded messages and curious symbols.

Maybe I was being welcomed. But to where? To what?

Maybe it was just a coincidence, another strange moment to laugh off. Or maybe—just maybe—it was a calling.

Why This Matters

Tuning into subtle signs and spiritual messages can open you to a more purposeful and connected life. It's through awareness of the uncanny that we begin to hear the voice of destiny and remember that life speaks in a language only our soul can understand.

Think back to a moment that felt like more than coincidence—something odd, symbolic, or surreal that stayed with you. What might it have been calling you toward? Are there messages you've ignored that you're now ready to understand?

8613 Hollywood Boulevard before the plants.

CHAPTER XV
Messages We Forget, Signs We Remember

This chapter invites us to consider that life is saturated with messages—subtle, symbolic, and often dismissed. From electronic signals to animal messengers to synchronistic events, it suggests that the universe is in constant communication with those willing to listen.

All day, all sorts of information—from letters to words, music, and videos—pass through our bodies via the wireless internet, radio waves, and other unidentified sources. But don't you think that information of all sorts has always been and is constantly being given to us "wirelessly"? If our receptors were sensitive enough, we could—and one day probably will—decipher these signals without any mechanical device doing the interpretation. We already know there's error in interpretation; it doesn't matter how accurate the understanding is.

At one point, I received so many signs I started calling my friend Barb Mansbridge every time something occurred. During one conversation, I told her they were happening so often and so fast she wouldn't believe it. But just as quickly as they occur, they're forgotten. So I called her every time. Within a day, she finally said, "OKAY, enough, stop calling!" If she was irritated by a few phone calls, imagine how it feels to be bombarded day and night.

Start looking around your life for signs. You might be surprised how many you'll receive. Trust your instincts. There are drawbacks, though. Be careful, and be aware that knowledge without purpose will drive a person mad.

My primitive theory on how humanity survives this deluge of knowledge without purpose is that insanity is actually the ability to forget. It is our greatest gift for survival and, at the same time, the very engine of our failure as a species.

Memory failure is the key to our endurance, yet it may also be the cause of our eventual collapse as a civilization. Imagine if we had all the answers to the universe instantly. The stress would be too much—we'd have the lifespan of a mayfly.

A couple of years later, on the anniversary of my father's death, I received a notice from a mortuary urging me to get my affairs in order. I was only forty-eight years old and in excellent health. Why would a mortuary be soliciting me?

In October 2010, in Palm Springs, two years after my father passed, I came home from work and gathered my mail. In it was a court notice. It couldn't be good news, though I hadn't broken any laws. I opened it: a notice to appear for jury duty. Strange, considering I'm not a U.S. citizen and therefore ineligible.

I chuckled and set the envelope aside. Minutes later, I called my mother to say hello. After some small talk, she told me that my father—dead two years—had received a jury duty notice too. Coincidence or a message?

The final story for this chapter also happened in Hawaii. I've already described my nightly walks to Magic Island near Waikiki. At first, I didn't even know the name of the park I was sitting in. But once I started telling my Hawaiian friends these stories and where they happened, my friend Keoni said, "That makes sense—it's called Magic Island. Magical things happen there."

I'd begun noticing the abundance of doves in places like Palm Springs, Waikiki, and Honolulu. So I looked up their symbolic meaning. The dove represents innocence, gentleness, faith, peace, constancy, and even marital affection.

In Christian lore, the dove symbolizes the Holy Spirit or a heavenly messenger. It appears in the Annunciation, and again when the Spirit descends upon Christ at his baptism: "He saw the Spirit of God descending like a dove to alight upon Him…" (Matthew 3:16 17). Later in Matthew 10:16, "Be wary as serpents, innocent as doves," ties the creature to gentleness and awareness.

The dove is a messenger of peace, its presence a balm to the troubled soul. In quiet moments, we find renewal through its symbolism—reminders that hope, miracles, and new beginnings are always within reach.

One afternoon, as I sat watching the sun dip toward the horizon and listening to the ocean's rhythm, a dove landed at my feet. I didn't overthink it; it pecked around in the dirt and then flew away.

But seconds later, it came back—with another dove. Then another. Then several more. And before long, nearly thirty doves were circling and cooing at my feet.

I moved my feet gently, expecting them to scatter, but they didn't. They kept pecking and walking around. Curious onlookers stopped to watch, their expressions echoing my own amazement.

Then just as suddenly, they all flew off together.

I chuckled again and whispered aloud, to no one and to every force that might have been listening, "What was that all about?"

Why This Matters

Learning to recognize and honor the signs around you can transform confusion into clarity and isolation into connection. It shifts your experience from randomness to revelation, helping you embrace a more attuned and spiritually awake life.

What signs or symbols have shown up repeatedly in your life? How have you interpreted them—or overlooked them? Reflect on a recent moment that might have carried a more profound message. What might it be trying to tell you?

CHAPTER XVI
A Voice Too Soon

This chapter explores signs as sacred echoes—threads woven between the natural and the supernatural, drawing your awareness toward the Divine. It shows that signs aren't always answers, but invitations to remember, to trust, and to awaken.

— For those times when you name what others aren't ready to hear, even if it's exactly what they need.

Life offers us many signs if we learn how to see them. Some are subtle nudges in the quiet corners of our hearts. Others scream across our path like neon revelations. The most obvious are those found in the perfection of nature: the position of the Earth, the breathability of the atmosphere, the miracle of consciousness. To believe these conditions happened by accident seems far less rational than to trust in something greater.

I have no issue with evolution as an ongoing process. It makes sense to me. But I take pause at the scientific community's confident claims about how it all began (the Big Bang) and how it all ends (with nothing). What if there is more? What if every moment—every flicker of insight, every unexplained sensation, every coincidence—is part of something more deliberate?

Back in my Hollywood Hills apartment, the walls themselves began to whisper truths. Apparitions appeared during my early morning showers, as though the water unlocked another frequency. Nearly every day, new images surfaced, joined by a deep, sweet fragrance—something like roses or cherries, but not quite either. I Googled the phenomenon and came across a forum post:

"The rose smell is one of your guides' ways of letting you know they are with you."

That stayed with me.

Remember the hotel light that would flicker every time I passed. It wasn't random—it pulsed, like Morse code from the beyond. I even stopped and spoke to it. Of course, it never replied with words.

It simply blinked. And once I passed, it stopped.

Then came the streetlights. Walking or driving, they would shut off as I neared, then come back on once I'd gone. It still happens. To others, these are coincidences. But once you start noticing, once you start *asking* for signs and actually *getting them*—that changes you.

When I asked the ALL for a sign, something always happened. Not sometimes—always.

Let me give you some examples.

The most overt sign happened shortly before I left Hollywood for Corbyville in 2008. I was alone in my apartment, in a kind of meditative trance, when a pure light appeared—not from any bulb or device, but *a light of life itself*. It wasn't physical, but I saw it as clearly as anything. The knowledge it imparted wasn't through words but *understanding*. It told me: Christ was with me. Not as a man in a robe, but as a *consciousness*. A field. A presence.

At first, I wondered if I *was* Him. Not from ego, but from awe. But then I realized: I was simply part of Him, walking with Him. A sliver of the Divine, asked to carry light in a dark time.

And just then, I felt something run down my face. I touched my forehead. Blood. A red line from the center of my brows downward. But there was no wound. No pain. Just blood. This was not imagination.

Later that year, I climbed a fence with sharp iron bars—one of those foolish decisions we make—and I slipped. A bar punctured my side. Later, I realized: it was exactly where Christ was pierced on the cross.

Add to that a surgery I'd had near the same spot, and recurring blisters in the center of my palms that would come and go, replaced by a burning sensation. Now, I'm not claiming I bear the wounds of Christ. But I am saying: the parallels are striking. When taken together, they suggest something *beyond chance*.

Water was another messenger.

One night, I returned to the bathroom. In the center of the floor: a pool of clear water. No leaks. No dripping faucets. No explanation. The next night, the same. It happened again and again. I dipped my fingers into it. Cold. Pure. I tasted it. Spring water—exactly like the creek behind my childhood home.

That was the water of anointment. Of cleansing. Of blessing.

There was more. One scorching Palm Springs afternoon, I returned to my car and found a single dead leaf at the driver's side door. Surrounding the curled leaf was a glistening pool of water. No sprinklers. No rain. Just water, cradled in death.

And the shower—the one in my Hollywood Hills apartment—that was something else entirely. Massive and made of stone, it became a sacred chamber. I'd take steam baths and see visions on the walls. They wouldn't photograph. I tried. I bought supplies to draw them. I couldn't capture them.

But one image—which I named "Peggy"—stayed with me. After seeing her, I heard a conversation between my parents from decades earlier. Crystal clear. Time bent in that room.

That shower gave me more than messages. It gave healing.

A friend from Palm Springs, gravely ill from a botched heart surgery, came to visit. Before his operation, I insisted he use my shower. I believed in its power. He scoffed, but he humored me.

The next morning, he had the surgery. Doctors were not optimistic. But he came through brilliantly—sitting up and laughing the next day.
I don't need to prove any of this. I only need to *remember*. That's what we're here to do, isn't it?

We forget. Then the Divine reminds.

Signs aren't just messages. They are *echoes of eternity*, reaching through time and perception to awaken us. They are the language of God. And once you hear it—really hear it—you can never unhear it again.

You only have one task: pay attention.

Why This Matters

When you begin to notice signs, you also begin to recognize your dialogue with the Divine. This awareness shifts your perception, deepens your faith, and grounds your life in meaning—even when logic has no explanation.

Have you ever received a sign that changed the way you saw your life or your place in the world? What do you think it was trying to tell you? Reflect on how you might stay open to more messages hidden in the ordinary moments around you.

CHAPTER XVII
Please, Don't Shoot the Messenger

This chapter shines light on the power—and the burden—of being a messenger. It explores the mysterious responsibility of intuition and premonition, reminding us that the truth isn't always welcome, but still necessary to speak.

No one told me my thoughts might be dangerous. People would say, "Think before you speak," but no one ever explained why. That advice—like counting to ten when you're angry—seemed incomplete. I tried it. Counted. Then got mad anyway. They forgot the essential part: the *why*. The truth is, by the time you reach ten, your anger has softened. The current has passed. So maybe, just maybe, the missing piece is time.

As I got older, I realized most of what I blurted out wasn't just awkward or mistimed—it was exposing things. Naming the unspoken. Premonitions, even. Words spoken in jest that echoed as prophecy. I never meant to stir trouble. But what do you do when the truth insists on slipping from your lips?

There was one time in the mid-1980s, when I lived in West Hollywood, that I made an offhand joke that turned into something else. I was hanging with friends, the usual twenty-something chaos of cheap drinks and too-loud music. Our rented house was the neighborhood eyesore, nestled among manicured lawns and upward mobility. One neighbor, in particular, loathed us. She'd invested in new landscaping, while our lawn looked like a scene from *Animal House*. One night, we laughed about her. I joked, "Someone should go hack down her new hedge." It got the desired chuckle, and that was that.

Until the next morning.

Her hedges had been hacked to bits. Gaping holes, limbs on the sidewalk, the whole thing. We stood there stunned. Then someone remembered my joke from the night before, and suddenly, all eyes were on me. I laughed—a nervous, shocked laugh. I hadn't touched a leaf. But from that day on, some friends called me "Hedda Hedgehacker."

Another time, working at an accounting firm in Beverly Hills, I joked with our receptionist about her beat-up VW Bug always breaking down. I said, "I should drive it into a sketchy neighborhood and let someone torch it so you can get a new one." Everyone laughed. The next morning? The car had been stolen and found smashed to pieces. Cue the slow turn of heads toward me.

I'd like to say I learned my lesson, but the truth is, messages don't stop just because you become more careful. They find new ways in. Over time, I began to see it wasn't about coincidence. I was receiving something. Transmission. Insight. Call it what you like. And I was supposed to share it.

The challenge was: how do you deliver messages when people shoot the messenger?

Words have weight. Timing has power. And most people don't want their illusions interrupted. They want the truth *later*, preferably after they've lived a little longer in denial. What I learned is that wisdom without tact is often treated as a threat.

After New York, in the middle of an economic collapse, I followed another internal nudge to Palm Springs. I landed a job at a boutique hotel called the Andreas. The manager, Charlie Robles, took a chance on me. I was broke, scraping by, and living on my friend Daryl's porch. But I kept showing up.

Years later, I learned that Ron Ogulnick, a name from my past accounting job in Beverly Hills, was now a co-owner of that very hotel. Synchronicity. Again.

One day, while painting in Daryl's driveway, I spilled some acrylic paint. I grabbed the hose to wash it off. The water easily removed most of the splatters—except one. A single blob of paint resisted. Water hit it directly, but it didn't budge. It didn't even get wet. It was like the laws of physics didn't apply to that one spot. I stood there, dumbfounded.

Sometimes, signs don't come in thunder or fire. Sometimes, they're a stubborn dot of paint. A hedge. A stolen car. A name that returns twenty years later.

I was compelled to ship my car from Hawaii to Los Angeles and drove to the Notre-Dame Basilica of Montreal. Looking for answers. Why there I have no idea. I am not even Catholic. A priest told me that divine messages are always personal. They don't come to impress the masses. They come to move the one who is ready. That's why prophets speak in parables. That's why truth is often mistaken for madness.

So, please, don't shoot the messenger because you don't like the message.

Why This Matters

Being in tune with unseen currents of insight requires courage, humility, and discernment. Sharing truth, especially when it challenges comfort, demands both boldness and sensitivity. Learning to honor messages without forcing them is part of spiritual maturity.

Have you ever felt compelled to say something others weren't ready to hear? How did it affect you—and them? Reflect on how you might better honor and deliver messages that come through you with wisdom and grace.

CHAPTER XVIII
The Four Faces of God

This chapter invites us to contemplate the archetypal dimensions of the Divine through ancient symbols—the Four Faces of God. It reveals that within us lies the prophet, the king, the servant, and the eternal spirit, reminding us of the power and responsibility we hold as reflections of the ALL.

Ezekiel 1:1-10

In the thirtieth year, on the fifth day of the fourth month, as Ezekiel stood among the exiles by the River Chebar, the heavens opened and visions of the ALL burst forth. Out of a whirlwind came a fire unfolding itself, glowing like amber, and from the fire emerged four living beings—each with four faces: that of a man, a lion, an ox, and an eagle. These are not to be taken literally. Their faces are symbols. They represent facets of the Divine within us all.

The Face of a Man — the prophet. Christ, the Son of Man, who walked among us, felt our pain, and bore our afflictions. It is the face of empathy, of suffering, of incarnation.

The Face of a Lion — the king. The Lion of Judah, royal and unyielding. It is Christ as conqueror, as divine authority. Strength. Command. The call to rise.

The Face of an Ox — the servant. The beast of burden. The one who carries, who labors, who sacrifices. Christ the humble, who washed feet and bore the weight of humanity.

The Face of an Eagle — the father. The guardian of heights. The visionary. The one who soars above and sees all. Majesty. Mystery. The breath of eternity.

In these four faces, we find the whole: the suffering servant, the conquering king, the humble laborer, and the eternal spirit. These archetypes are not distant—they are within.

All four found on the wall of the shower.

And just as these four faces appear, so too do the Four Horsemen of Revelation: Conquest, War, Famine, and Death. Together, they ride forth, ushering in the end. Or perhaps, transformation.

The white horse rides first. Crowned, bow in hand. Conquest, or perhaps the false light of the Antichrist.

Then the red horse—War. Civil unrest. Strife.

The third, black as famine. The scale tips. Hunger rises.

And the final pale horse. Death rides. And with him, Hades.

These are not fictions. They are the truths we feel—the storms that pass through the soul of humanity. But just as there are horsemen, there are also angels. There is always the ALL.

Why This Matters

Recognizing the Divine within deepens our relationship with both ourselves and the cosmos. It empowers us to navigate life not merely as seekers, but as embodied aspects of wisdom, strength, humility, and vision.

Which of the Four Faces—Man, Lion, Ox, Eagle—do you most recognize in yourself right now? Which one feels furthest away? Reflect on how each archetype might help you grow, lead, serve, and ascend.

CHAPTER XIX
Where Will You Spend Eternity?

This chapter centers around the question that echoes through all spiritual seeking: Where will you spend eternity? But rather than pointing to fear or dogma, it gently leads us toward awakened recognition through synchronicity, scripture, and the mysterious language of signs.

By now, you either believe the signs—or you don't. But if you look back through your life, really *look*, you'll find them. Once one rises from memory, others flood through. The past lights up like a constellation.

It may sound like I lounge around channel surfing, and I probably do more than I should. But in that quiet space, my subconscious often solves what my conscious mind cannot.

One evening, flipping through the channels, I landed on TMZ—yes, that trashy, tabloid TV show known for stalking celebrities. On that episode, the camera crew approached a football star I'd never heard of—Tim Tebow. They asked, "What's your favorite Bible verse?"
Without hesitation, he answered, "John 3:16."

That name meant nothing to me. I didn't know the reference. But something compelled me to look it up. I went to Google, my modern oracle, and typed in: "John 3:16."

I found dozens of translations:

"For God so loved the world, that He gave His only begotten Son, that whoever believes in Him should not perish, but have everlasting life."

Each translation slightly different. But the message always the same.
I didn't understand why this moment mattered—until the next day.

Daryl, a friend, had a client to visit in downtown Palm Springs. I tagged along. While he went inside, I waited out in the scorching sun. I found a ledge for shade, and when I sat, there it was—a coin.

It looked like a silver dollar. But as I picked it up, I realized it was plastic. A toy. But on one side, printed in tiny letters, was John 3:16.

The verse I'd just learned the night before. Coincidence? No. Synchronicity. Yes.

These moments used to pass me by. I'd laugh or shrug and forget. But over time, I've learned to pay attention. To look deeper. And every time I do, something in me opens. Some connection lights up.

The Divine speaks in whispers and symbols. If we ignore them, they don't stop—they just wait. So I ask again: Where will you spend eternity? Not in fear. But in truth. Not in blind belief. But in awakened recognition. The signs are here. Now, what will you do with them?

Why This Matters

Acknowledging the presence of a higher intelligence guiding your journey can inspire reverence and introspection. It invites you to see your life as part of a sacred tapestry—one woven with grace, invitation, and eternal belonging.

Have you ever experienced a moment so aligned or symbolic it felt like a divine wink? Reflect on how synchronicity has shaped your view of purpose or eternity. What message might be waiting for you, if you're willing to listen?

Picture of actual coin, that I still have twenty years later.

Headline: The trace of a man's face. Photo supplied by Google.

This chapter closes the journey with a reminder that life, like a river, flows with mystery, pain, purpose, and grace. It teaches that healing comes through connection—both to the earth beneath our feet and the soul within our being—and that synchronicity is not random, but a guidepost for the sacred.

Even as I write this final chapter, stranger-than-fiction moments continue to unfold. My story remains bewildering—why me? Why since childhood, and likely until my last breath? Despite everything, my secular mind still questions the validity of these spiritual happenings. Is this the human voyage? Will it take lifetimes to understand? Or is this it—the only lifetime, the only chance?

The image above is of the Moira River. My grandmother wrote about it. On August 31, 2011, my mother called to tell me the image was pictured in the Belleville Intelligencer. These seemingly small occurrences carry hidden depth, like echoes of past lives speaking through time.

Between 2008 and 2012, my life unraveled and illuminated in equal measure. I lost my father. My career dissolved. My savings vanished. I was practically homeless, jobless, and watching the world suffer a financial meltdown. What is a man—fifty years old—to do? The answer: don't lose faith. I didn't. In fact, faith grew.

Instead of mourning what I lost, I began to give thanks for what I still had. Through it all, I sensed the ALL—the presence of divine order—still lighting my path. I prayed daily for strength, wisdom, and clarity. I asked for the courage to see my destiny clearly and to follow its light.

I searched tirelessly for work. I've never been above any job. In fact, work gives me purpose and keeps my spirit engaged. During this time, I leaned on friends—those who offered not just support, but dignity.

One day, I sat in a coffee shop hoping to hear of work through word-of-mouth. My phone rang. A woman on the line had seen my résumé online. We talked for a few minutes, and then she asked, "Is this Chris, Daryl James' friend?" I said yes, surprised. I didn't recognize her name, but her voice stirred a memory.

We ended the call, thinking there wasn't a good job fit. A few hours later, she called again. Another position had come up—finance related. That's when I remembered her: she and her partner had once visited Daryl's house.
Back then, the man she was with—Clint Ober—was barefoot in the garden, explaining how diseases stem from our disconnection from Earth's energy. He introduced the concept of "earthing." Daryl saw marketing potential. I, however, dismissed it.

But now, years later, here I was interviewing for a role at Earthing.com.

Synchronicity. Destiny.

While working for the company, I began reflecting on what disconnection truly means. If humanity is cut off from the Earth's healing energy—its electrons—how can we hope to connect to anything higher? How can we touch the soul if we've lost contact with the soles of our feet?

The Earth is not just ground—it's a gateway.

Touching it, barefoot, is the first step back to our source. Sole to soul. That's the path.

Reconnection with nature realigns the body's energy and calms the mind. When we are physically grounded, we can become spiritually attuned. It's not a new truth. But sometimes we need new ways to remember it.

Take the first step. Put your feet on the earth. Pray with gratitude. Let your body heal. Let your soul remember.

I have one last story, in case you still doubt synchronicity, divine intelligence, or destiny.

In February 2011, my friend Jane threw herself a sixtieth birthday party in Hollywood. Extravagant, joyful, and wonderfully over-the-top—complete with clowns, pantomimes, and stilt walkers. Jane never does anything halfway.

During the party, I sat for a tarot card reading. I've had readings before. Most said the same: I'm a dreamer, I live with my head in the clouds, I'll settle down late in life. But this time, the reader looked at me and said something no one else ever had:

"You're a very grounded person." And she emphasized the word: grounded. Grounded—at the very time I was literally working in the field of grounding.

Coincidence? No. Another sign.

Okay, one last story. This one lingered in my inbox for nearly a year before I decided to share it. It's personal. It's about healing.

The year was 1977. I was fifteen, surrounded by the pressures of adolescence, financial strain, and a crowded household. My escape was television. One show in particular—Eight is Enough—became a kind of emotional sanctuary.

In a Christmas episode called Yes, Nicholas, There Is a Santa Claus, the family, still grieving the loss of their mother, faces another blow: their house is robbed. The character Tommy, who was around my age, struggled the most. But in the end, his new stepmother finds a hidden gift from his late mother—a symbol of her enduring love.

The family gathers. Tommy softens. And the message is clear: love binds us. Family matters.

I was in a raw emotional state. Then, just as the scene reached its heartfelt peak, a real-life argument exploded in my home. I was yanked out of that tender moment by screaming and was sent to bed. My emotions—wide open—were trampled. A wound formed.

I carried that scar for decades.

Flash forward to 2009. Alec Baldwin was doing Hulu ads, and I stumbled upon the site. I watched some old favorites. Then, I remembered that episode.

I searched endlessly until I found it. I watched it—this time in peace. I cried. I healed. The wound closed.

A few weeks later, I tried to find it again. It was gone.

Just like everything else in this journey—it came when I needed it. Then vanished. Like the river, my story rambles on. But unlike the river, I know it has a source—and a destination.

Stay open. Stay grounded. Stay awake.

Why This Matters

Embracing the ebb and flow of life deepens your resilience and spiritual awareness. Grounding yourself—literally and metaphorically—can become a path of restoration, clarity, and divine alignment. The more you remember, the more you heal.

What moments in your life felt like the river was speaking to you— guiding or healing you? How has grounding, in nature or memory, helped restore your connection to spirit? What is one sacred sign or experience you now understand more clearly?

Willie Aames as Tommy

Did the episode play just long enough to help me heal?

GOD DOES WORK IN MYSTERIOUS WAYS!

CHAPTER XXI
Alchemy: A Metaphysical Metaphor

This chapter explores the ancient art of alchemy as a powerful metaphor for personal transformation. It teaches that the fire of our deepest questions—especially "Why?"—becomes the forge that purifies, reshapes, and awakens our soul.

The echo of "Whyyyyyyy?" bounced off the walls of my mother's birth canal the moment I emerged into the world—swiftly smacked on the backside, gasping for air. WHY!? The best answer I ever got over the years. "Just because."

"Just because" never cut it. With all the beauty, pain, and mystery of life—was that really all there was to it? That feeble answer always struck me as either dishonest or uninformed. And so I asked again. And again. And again. My search for meaning began in protest. If no one else could give me a good answer, I would find it myself.

So began the journey of Why.

Why are we here? Why am I here? Why this body? Why this timeline? Why this family? Why this struggle? Why this yearning? Why the knowing I couldn't explain? Why the pull toward something beyond what the world could see?

I began to notice patterns—some people were always asking what, others asked how, when, or where. But me? I asked why. That became my signature, my soul print. And in asking why, I began to uncover who I was.

From an early age, I was drawn to the elements—earth, air, fire, water, and especially ether. Ether felt sacred, secret, and limitless. I didn't fully understand it, but I knew it existed. Just hearing the word made me feel wiser, older, more ancient than my years.

Despite a standard North American education, I sensed a deeper truth that was missing. I was solid in my ABCs, math, and geography. But something felt... recycled. Taught, but not lived. Memorized, but not understood. "Because that's how it's always been," they'd say. And I'd sigh. Not good enough.

It was the power of Why that led me inward. That prompted my self-examination. That carved out a path toward self-realization. I came to understand—sometimes with clarity, sometimes in confusion—that asking why the path is. That we walk it not to reach a final answer, but to become the kind of soul who dares to ask at all.

According to an old Chinese proverb, enlightenment "is a direction, not a destination." And in every step, breath, beat, and breakdown, I have moved further along that direction.

So how did this tie into alchemy?

One day, while researching the Akashic Records for my thesis, a video documentary popped up in my YouTube recommendations: Alchemy: Sacred Secrets Revealed by Luxor Media. I clicked. Not coincidence—synchronicity. The kind I'd come to trust.

The film described alchemy not just as the ancient quest to transform base metals into gold, but as a metaphor for metaphysical transformation—our spiritual evolution from lead to light.

The word alchemy itself comes from two Greek roots: "al," meaning "the," and "khemet," referring to Egypt's black fertile soil. Black soil, black magic. Creation rising from darkness.

Alchemy is linked to Thoth, Egyptian god of wisdom and magic, who eventually merged mythologically with Hermes to become Hermes Trismegistus—a Master of Science, math, medicine, and mysticism. The foundational text of alchemy, the Emerald Tablet, is attributed to him.

The Tablet is poetic, cryptic, multilayered. It declares:

"That which is below is like that which is above, and that which is above is like that which is below."

This is the law of correspondence. The macrocosm and the microcosm. Heaven and Earth. Mind and matter. All reflecting each other in sacred symmetry.

Some say the Tablet was discovered beneath a statue of Hermes in Tyana, placed on a golden throne, held by a centuries-old corpse. True or not, the metaphor is clear: wisdom lives beneath the surface. It awaits our digging, our death to the old, our rebirth into the new.

Over the centuries, some of the greatest minds studied alchemy—not just to change metal, but to understand the soul: Pythagoras, Plato, Galileo, Newton. Plato imagined a future where all men would become philosophers, their souls golden like the sun.

Isaac Newton's translation of the Emerald Tablet reads:

"Its force is entire if it be turned into earth. Separate the earth from the fire, the subtle from the gross, sweetly, with great industry. It ascends from the earth to the heaven, and descends again to the earth… By this means you shall have the glory of the whole world."

In other words: transformation is a cycle. Rise. Descend. Integrate.

Repeat.

So where does this leave us?

Alchemy is not just ancient. It's alive in us. The nigredo—the dark night of the soul. The albedo—awakening. The rubedo—illumination.

Consciousness, in this metaphor, is the fire that transmutes our leaden thoughts into golden truths. It is the spark of divine remembrance.

Alchemy teaches us that transformation is not just possible—it is inevitable when we surrender to the process. Our job is not to understand everything, but to say yes to the journey.

We are not here to "just because."

We are here to become.

So was the world created.

Why This Matters

In a world of distraction and surface answers, the courage to ask
"Why?" and to seek real meaning sets us on a sacred path. Alchemy is
not just about transformation—it is about wholeness, remembering
that everything below mirrors what is above, and vice versa.

What is your personal "why"? What deep question has shaped your
journey? Reflect on how your pain, longing, or confusion may be the
raw material for your spiritual gold.

CHAPTER XXII
Conscious-centered Living
Calling Everything into Question

This chapter asks us to bring everything—philosophy, spirituality, science, and daily life—into conscious awareness. It reminds us that questioning is the path to depth, not distraction, and that awareness is the fertile soil in which meaning and transformation grow.

"To be aware or not to be aware, that is the question!" A playful twist on Hamlet's famous existential pondering humorously introduces a deeply significant inquiry. Indeed, living consciously brings forth profound existential questions: "Who am I?" "Why do I exist?" "What is my life's purpose?" "Why do we suffer?" Such questions have echoed throughout humanity's history and will continue to resonate as long as humans reflect upon existence.

Consciousness has long sparked fierce debates among philosophers, scientists, and mystics alike. Despite exhaustive intellectual analysis, definitions remain elusive. Reason alone proves insufficient; consciousness is inherently experiential, requiring intuition and sensation alongside logical thought for a holistic understanding.

Philosophically, reason stands as the logical inference process, distinct from intuition, feeling, and sensation—faculties empiricists historically question. Questioning itself becomes a catalyst for self-reflection and awareness. It is understandable, then, why perspectives diverge dramatically, with some celebrating consciousness exploration while others dismiss it outright.

Western philosophical traditions grapple with consciousness's enigmatic relationship to matter, language, technology, and selfhood. Key debates explore whether consciousness can manifest in artificial intelligence, how language shapes consciousness, and whether consciousness itself is coherent or inherently paradoxical.

Yet, practical considerations remain paramount: what does conscious-centered living truly entail? Amidst global strife and personal turmoil, humanity seeks refuge, peace, and joy. Frequently, individuals pursue these through religious paths, philosophies, and teachers, seeking permanence in transient experiences. But is true happiness rooted in permanence, or is everything merely a derivative of an ineffable eternal truth?

Language matters profoundly in this exploration. Words shape our reality, serving as both bridges and barriers to understanding consciousness. Despite extensive literature and research, genuine consciousness remains deeply personal and experiential rather than purely intellectual. Thus arises the crucial question: How can we authentically cultivate consciousness in ourselves, individually and collectively?

Consciousness is now an interdisciplinary pursuit encompassing psychology, neuroscience, anthropology, linguistics, and metaphysics. Scientific studies measure consciousness through subjective verbal reporting and medical observations, from alertness to deep coma states. The overwhelming influx of digital information further complicates modern understanding, posing both opportunities and challenges.

Ancient wisdom, ranging from The Kybalion to Egyptian metaphysics, offers rich perspectives on consciousness and human purpose. Conversely, modern philosophical and psychological explorations, such as those by Carl Jung, Jordan Peterson, and various metaphysical institutions, continue to expand understanding.

Historically, humanity's understanding of consciousness has evolved dramatically through eras marked by cultural flourishing and turmoil— from Classical Antiquity and the Medieval period through the Renaissance, Enlightenment, Industrial Revolutions, and modern technological advances. Each era has shaped human perception, consciousness, and identity uniquely, contributing to contemporary dialogues.

Storytelling profoundly influences consciousness, suggesting our lives are either random or predetermined narratives. This duality fuels existential anxieties intensified by unprecedented access to information and yet persistent comprehension challenges in our digital age.

Ultimately, conscious-centered living invites constant questioning and self-reflection. Embracing this ongoing inquiry enriches personal growth and collective evolution. By consciously engaging life's profound mysteries, humanity moves toward deeper awareness, compassion, and fulfillment.

Consciousness & Self-consciousness

Some philosophers and spiritual traditions have argued that the mind and body are separate entities. René Descartes notably advocated dualism—the belief that the mind is an independent, non-material entity distinct from the physical body. Conversely, modern psychologists view consciousness as inherently rooted in the neural activity of the brain, influenced by countless interconnections shaping its varied manifestations. At its core, consciousness involves awareness of both internal states and external realities.

Consciousness has been described in diverse ways, from simple wakefulness to profound explorations of the self or soul. It can be experienced as a flowing stream of thoughts, a mental event, or the intimate sense of what it feels like "to be."

As Carl Jung noted, consciousness evolved slowly through history, and its development remains ongoing, with large areas of the human mind yet unexplored. Modern research explores consciousness in various dimensions: from organic to non-organic, individual perception to collective synchronicities, and even into quantum physics.

Philosopher Jiddu Krishnamurti highlights consciousness as comprising the entirety of one's inner landscape, including thoughts, desires, fears, joys, and inspirations. Consciousness extends beyond the immediate awareness into subconscious realms, accessible through dreams, intuition, or profound reflection. Conflict arises when consciousness is fragmented; true harmony emerges when we cultivate holistic awareness.

Neville Goddard characterizes consciousness through the interplay of conscious (masculine) and subconscious (feminine) aspects, with the conscious mind selective and personal, while the subconscious is universal and non-selective. Understanding this dynamic relationship enables deeper comprehension of oneself and reality.

Why This Matters

In a world overwhelmed by noise, conscious-centered living becomes a radical and sacred act. It offers a way to reclaim your sovereignty and develop inner clarity, wisdom, and purpose. The more you question with sincerity, the more you awaken to life's invisible architecture.

What does it mean for you to live consciously? How might deeper awareness reshape your relationships, your beliefs, or your sense of self? Reflect on one area of your life where bringing more awareness might create healing or transformation.

CHAPTER XXIII
Awakening the Inner Oracle From Self-Consciousness to Synchronicity

This chapter expands the journey into self-consciousness and synchronicity, emphasizing that we are both observers and creators of our reality. By cultivating conscious awareness, we gain access to deeper truths, intuitive insights, and a clearer connection to the quantum fabric of life.

Self-consciousness refers to the awareness of oneself as both subject and object. Initially synonymous with self-awareness, modern interpretations often distinguish self-consciousness as heightened sensitivity to how others perceive us, manifesting as social anxiety, embarrassment, or shyness. While this heightened awareness can foster growth and self-understanding, excessive self-consciousness can impair confidence and self-esteem.

Psychologists differentiate between private self-consciousness—internal introspection—and public self-consciousness, reflecting concern about external perceptions. These traits significantly influence behavior and identity formation, often becoming more apparent in situations that alter perceptions of anonymity or visibility.

In the poetic wisdom of Kahlil Gibran, self-knowledge emerges from deep inner silence and intuition, rather than from external validation or superficial judgments. The soul's depth is limitless, unfolding naturally like a lotus. Gibran advises us to approach self-discovery humbly, recognizing truth as multifaceted and individual journeys as unique paths traversed by the soul.

Synchronicity represents the conscious merging of parallel realities, revealing a deeper understanding of life's interconnected phenomena. As humans elevate their self-awareness and connect more profoundly with their higher minds, the tapestry of existence increasingly reveals itself through meaningful coincidences and purposeful alignments. This awareness aligns with quantum physics' revelations about the quantum field, which intrinsically binds all separate entities into a singular, connected whole.

Human consciousness is not merely an observer but an active participant in reality's formation. Neville Goddard encapsulates this notion powerfully: "Consciousness is the only reality." According to Goddard, the reality we experience directly mirrors our internal states and convictions. Florence Scovel Shinn complements this idea by emphasizing the power of impressing the subconscious mind. The external world reflects our inner world—our beliefs, fears, and desires. Thus, by consciously directing our inner state, we transform our external experiences.

Living a conscious-centered lifestyle involves recognizing that we are continually shaping and reshaping reality through our awareness. Rather than seeing ourselves as passive entities subject to external forces, conscious living empowers us to recognize that consciousness itself is the primary cause behind life's phenomena. The shift from external causation to internal awareness frees us from external dependencies, highlighting the importance of nurturing our consciousness with positive intent.

Intuition plays a pivotal role as a spiritual faculty guiding this conscious-centered lifestyle. Unlike logic or reasoning, intuition directly taps into the quantum field's universal intelligence, providing insights without explicit explanations. Although philosophers like Daniel Dennett describe intuition as merely subconscious pattern recognition, its profound ability to point the way toward higher truths remains undeniable.

The ancient philosophical concept of eternal return reinforces the significance of consciously embracing life's continuous cycle of becoming. Life is an ever-evolving spiral of experiences, constantly shifting and reforming. Recognizing consciousness as the core element of existence allows us to accept these perpetual transformations with grace and intentionality.

Ultimately, a conscious-centered life is one of profound empowerment and interconnectedness. By intentionally directing our consciousness, embracing intuitive guidance, and acknowledging our unity with all existence, we step into a meaningful reality shaped deliberately by our awakened awareness. This conscious alignment is not merely philosophical; it is the practical foundation for a fulfilling, spiritually enriched life.

In this edition, we embark together on an intriguing journey into the captivating world of synchronicities—those meaningful coincidences that whisper deeper truths into our lives. We will explore both the synchronicities we readily understand and those mysterious events whose meanings are yet to be unveiled. Alongside these fascinating phenomena, we delve into profound concepts such as the Sacred Secretion, Reincarnation, Hermeticism, and Gnosis, each offering unique insights to enrich our understanding of existence.

Why This Matters

Living with self-conscious awareness transforms us from passive recipients of experience into active co-creators. Understanding how our thoughts shape reality, how synchronicities guide us, and how ancient and modern philosophies converge empowers us to engage life with purpose and clarity.

Reflect on a recent moment when your inner world clearly shaped your outer experience. How do you experience synchronicity? What is one way you can more consciously engage with your reality starting today?

CHAPTER XXIV
Circumambulation of the Soul

This chapter delves deeper into the phenomenon of synchronicity, illuminating its role as a guiding force on the path to self-realization. Through meaningful coincidences and symbolic encounters, synchronicity offers a dialogue between the conscious self and the mysterious intelligence of the universe.

What distinguishes this exploration is my personal and profound connection to the ancient land of Egypt, where synchronicities have guided me toward remarkable insights. Through sharing these experiences, I aim to spark your curiosity and encourage you to explore deeper into these intriguing realms. Prepare yourself for a thought-provoking and uplifting adventure!

This section pays homage to exceptional individuals whose unconventional and visionary approaches have profoundly reshaped our understanding of the world. From Hermes Trismegistus's cryptic wisdom to Carl Jung's insightful teachings, these figures are not merely historical—they serve as guiding mentors on our collective journey toward enlightenment. You, dear reader, play a pivotal role, for it is your curiosity and engagement that breathe life into this exploration.

Like renowned psychologist Carl Jung, my personal journey has been punctuated by uncanny and mysterious occurrences. At times, overwhelmed by these inexplicable phenomena, I feared for my sanity, prompting a deeper quest to uncover their significance within the framework of synchronicity. This personal exploration, echoing Jung's footsteps, provides a unique perspective that I'm eager and thrilled to share with you.

Jung coined the term "synchronicity" in 1930, describing meaningful coincidences without an apparent causal connection, which challenge our conventional understanding of the universe. Such synchronicities are integral to the process of individuation—our journey toward self-realization. Rather than linear progression, this transformative journey unfolds as a circumambulation around symbolic centers, such as mandalas, representing the divine pattern and the essence of the self.

A compelling illustration of synchronicity comes from Jung himself. A patient dreamt of receiving a golden scarab, a significant Egyptian symbol of rebirth, at a crucial moment during her therapy. As she shared this dream, Jung heard a tapping sound and discovered a beetle striking the window—a rare event precisely mirroring the patient's dream. This powerful coincidence shattered her rigid, rational defenses, marking a turning point in her therapeutic transformation.

These experiences of synchronicity invite us to recognize that life is interwoven by deeper meanings beyond conventional causality. Jung encourages us to remain open to these occurrences as reflections of our undiscovered inner selves. By attentively observing these phenomena, we gain profound insights that can guide us toward deeper self-awareness and transformation.

My personal journey since 2008 has continuously prompted a provocative question: "Why me?" Despite an initial skepticism toward spirituality and a rebellious youth spent rejecting conventional beliefs, a series of synchronistic events eventually awakened my curiosity about metaphysics and spirituality.

My journey resurged in earnest in 2014, rekindling my interest in hypnotherapy, which I first explored in 1986. This path eventually led me to formal studies in metaphysics at The University of Metaphysics and The University of Sedona, institutions embracing exploration without dogma. My education revealed a clear distinction between innate (gnostic) knowledge—arising from personal experiences and intuition—and indoctrinated knowledge imparted by external sources. Embracing both, while maintaining a critical perspective, has profoundly shaped my understanding of life's deeper mysteries.

You Never Know from Where or When

In the chapter titled "The Coming Home," I recount a remarkable encounter with a 90-year-old man on a golf course who spontaneously shared a story about my grandfather. Astonishingly, this story provided an answer to a lifelong question my brother John had posed just a day earlier, revealing the profound synchronicity connecting seemingly unrelated events.

Similarly, while practicing hypnotherapy in Ottawa in 2023, I met Tina, whose vibrant spirit immediately resonated with mine. Tina had just returned from a spiritual retreat in Costa Rica, seeking clarity about her transformative ayahuasca experiences. Months into our collaboration, she shared a YouTube video titled "The Sacred Secretion," discussing the pineal gland's spiritual significance. Initially skeptical, I soon realized this information marked a profound "aha" moment in my own spiritual awakening.

Tina's and the elderly man's stories serve as powerful reminders of synchronicity's role in our lives—revealing answers, connecting us deeply with others, and guiding us toward essential truths. Synchronicity reminds us that everything is interconnected, urging us always to remain open to life's unexpected yet deeply meaningful encounters.

Why This Matters

Recognizing synchronicities as more than mere chance empowers you to live with greater trust and openness. These moments of alignment often point the way when logic fails, reminding you that life is infused with hidden patterns and spiritual intelligence waiting to be noticed.

Think of a time when a "coincidence" seemed to speak directly to your inner question or struggle. What guidance did it offer? How might you invite more awareness of these patterns into your daily life?

CHAPTER XXV
Raising the Chrism

This chapter unveils the esoteric mystery of the Sacred Secretion—a spiritual process woven through the physical body and cosmic consciousness. It emphasizes that transformation is not merely symbolic, but a physiological and energetic alignment that reconnects us to divine awareness.

The Sacred Secretion: An Inner Resurrection

If you've read *The Anointment*, you already know that I didn't set out to write about the Sacred Secretion. The term itself surfaced almost prophetically—an uninvited guest whispering ancient truths into my waking consciousness. At the time, I had no intellectual framework for it. Just a knowing. A feeling. A visceral reaction in my body. Words like "oil," "birth," "Christ consciousness," and "solar plexus" swirled through my spirit like fragments of a forgotten language. It all seemed irrational—until it began to feel inevitable.

Let me start here: The Sacred Secretion is not mythology. It's not just metaphor. It is a physiological process—ancient, divine, and buried beneath centuries of religious dogma and scientific dismissal. It bridges mysticism and anatomy, scripture and biology, heaven and flesh.
It begins with a seed.

The Journey of the Christos Oil

In the center of our brain lies the cerebrum, a crown-like structure that houses the highest functions of human consciousness. In esoteric anatomy, this is the true "Holy of Holies." Within this upper chamber of thought and divinity, sacred elements are produced—namely a golden oil, called by some the "Christos," which descends the spinal column through the vagus nerve, symbolically echoing the journey of Jesus from the heavenly realms into earthly form.

This oil, this sacred secretion, makes its way down the spine and rests for 2.5 days in the solar plexus—Bethlehem, the "house of bread." Here, in this humble inner manger, the sacred seed waits. And if the conditions of your body and mind are aligned—meaning no intoxicants, stressors, or spiritual dissonance interfere—it rises. It ascends back up the spine, illuminating each chakra or energy center as it goes, until it reaches the pineal gland—Mount Pineal, or Mount Zion in symbolic scripture.

When this sacred oil returns upward, it is transfigured. Not dead, but amplified. Resurrected.

This is the mystical rebirth.

The Pineal Gland: Inner Stargate

What modern science knows about the pineal gland is both fascinating and incomplete. It is a small, pinecone-shaped gland located in the epithalamus of the brain, associated with the regulation of melatonin and circadian rhythm. But ancient wisdom tells us more. Much more.
This gland has long been revered as the "seat of the soul." In Egyptian mythology, it was symbolized by the Eye of Horus. In Eastern traditions, it corresponds to the Ajna chakra, or third eye—our portal to higher vision, divine intelligence, and inner knowing.

The pineal gland becomes activated when the Sacred Secretion completes its journey. Many mystics describe sensations of inner light, vivid dreams, euphoric peace, or flashes of spiritual insight at this stage. Others report a literal sweet taste in the mouth—a milk-and-honey-like secretion from the pituitary and pineal glands, symbolizing the promised land spoken of in scripture.

And yes—I've felt it. I've seen it. I wasn't dreaming. It was real.

This isn't metaphor. It's a biological sacrament.

My Body Became the Temple

I experienced a radiant pressure in my chest, as if something ancient and holy was returning to a place it had once known. The thymus gland pulsed with life. The heart raced, but not from fear—from recognition. Something within me had been activated.

And then there was the smell—roses. Sweet, rich, almost impossible to describe. It filled the room when no candles were lit, when no oils were burning. I later learned that this "scent of roses" has been reported for centuries during spiritual visitations. Some call it the perfume of angels. Others say it is the presence of Christ Consciousness itself.

Another time, blood ran down my forehead while in meditation. There was no wound. No pain. Just a red line, descending from the center of my brow, like stigmata.

And I did. Inwardly. Outwardly. Viscerally.

At first, I thought I was losing my mind. But in truth, I was finding it. Or more accurately—I was remembering it.

The Bible as Inner Map

Much of what's recorded in sacred texts is allegory. Not fiction. Not fable. But encoded truth.

The Virgin Birth is not merely a tale of miraculous conception—it is symbolic of the untouched, unpolluted seed within each of us. Christ is not just a man on a cross, but the divine consciousness born in every soul when the sacred oil is preserved, protected, and risen.

Joseph and Mary are not just parents—they are the pituitary and pineal glands. Bethlehem is the solar plexus. Golgotha, the place of the skull, is the higher brain. The resurrection? It's the return of the anointed oil to the cerebrum. And the ascension is not into clouds, but into divine awareness.

This is the inner gospel. The truth written not in ink, but in cells.

A Sacred Reminder

As Dr. George W. Carey wrote, "Man has turned his mighty power toward everything except himself—the greatest miracle of all."
When we turn inward, when we align our minds, bodies, and spirits, we activate this miracle. We stop looking outward for salvation and begin the sacred process of self-resurrection. This is not arrogance. It is

humility. It is realizing that we are not separate from the Divine—we are vessels of it.

In truth, the Sacred Secretion is not a "secret." It has been whispered in every tradition, etched into every temple, encoded into every myth. We simply forgot how to see it.

But now—we remember.

Bethlehem: The Solar Plexus where the sacred oil rests before resurrection.

Christos Oil The sacred oil or seed from the brain that descends and ascends the spine.

Solar Plexus Energy center of personal power, intuition, and spiritual rebirth.

Pineal Gland Third eye; center of spiritual vision and higher consciousness.

Golgotha The skull; symbolic site of the inner crucifixion and resurrection.

Joseph & Mary, The pituitary and pineal glands that produce spiritual 'fluids.'

Milk & Honey Spiritual nectar experienced during full awakening.

Cerebrum Upper brain chamber; symbolic of heaven or divine consciousness.

Spinal Column Pathway of energy and sacred fluid, connecting all chakras.

Mount Zion Crown chakra or summit of spiritual enlightenment.

Why This Matters

Understanding the Sacred Secretion invites us to reframe ancient spiritual texts and bodily experiences as part of a profound divine blueprint. It bridges science, mysticism, and personal revelation, offering us a path toward inner anointment and self-realization.

Have you experienced a physical or emotional awakening that seemed to hold deeper spiritual meaning? Reflect on your connection to your body as a sacred vessel. How might you honor the divine processes happening within you every day?

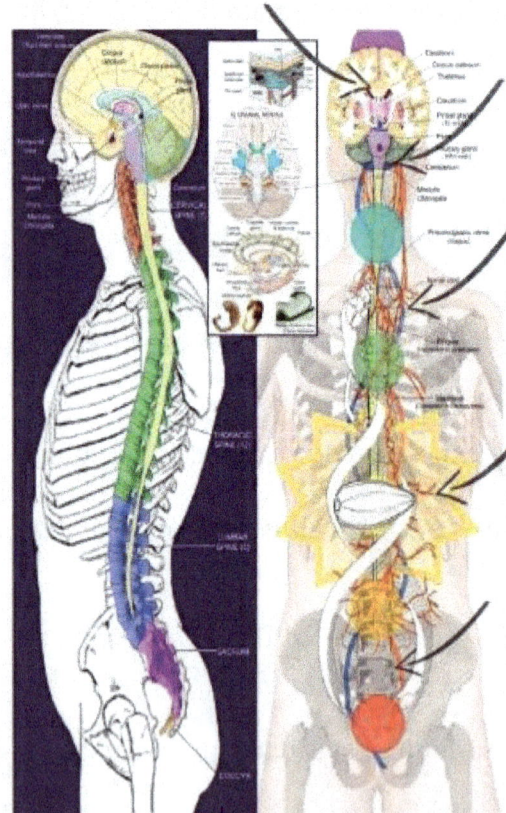

1. The Pineal Gland 'Joseph' secrets the milk, the Pituitary 'Mary' secrets the honey, both from the same source the Claustrum 'Santa Claus'.

RAISING THE CHRISM: SANTA CLAUS JOSEPH MARY AND THE CRUCIFICTION

5. The sacred oilr returns after the crossing 'the crucifiction' it enters the cerebellum 'Golgotha' the place of the skull. The fluid 'Christ'is refined 1000 x fold.

2. The two sacred oils travel down into the solar plexus via the semi-lunar ganglion Pneumogastric nerve

3. The Psycho-Physical Germ 'the Fruit of the Tree of Life' is born in the Solar Plexus 'the Manger'

4. The Ida (red), Pingala (blue), two nervw fluids where at the crossing of the medulla oblongata the crucifiction takes place where it rests for 2 and a half days.

https://clineapothecary.com

CHAPTER XXVI
The Numbers Know

In January 2024, I moved into a new apartment on Gilmour Street in Ottawa, Ontario, Canada. Before this fresh start, I had lived at 201 Metcalfe Street in apartments 25, 15, and finally 10, for two challenging years. The building itself seemed to reflect my increasingly difficult experience—it was sinking, neglected by management, becoming unsafe and unwelcoming. The negative energy within its walls was palpable, and I knew my time there had come to an end. It was a stark lesson in how quickly circumstances can shift, how one can move from being a landlord's ideal tenant to a perceived burden the moment usefulness fades.

The arrival of 2024 heralded more than just a new year; it signified a profound personal milestone. I was immediately greeted by remarkable synchronicities—signs I interpreted as positive affirmations of my decision.

One striking example of synchronicity lies in the concept of special birthdays—diamond, platinum, and golden—each with unique numerical alignments reflective of deeper life meanings. My Diamond birthday arrived precisely when my age matched the last two digits of my birth year. Born in 1962, my diamond birthday occurred as I turned 62, aligning numerically with remarkable precision: 6+2 equals 8, symbolizing infinity, abundance, and continuity.

My Platinum birthday had arrived years earlier, marking the time when my age mirrored my birth date flipped. Born on January 24, my platinum birthday came at 42 in 2004. That was the year my spiritual awakening intensified while living in Montreal, Quebec. The numbers again provided symbolic depth: 4+2 equaled 6, harmonizing beautifully with the year 2004 itself (2+0+0+4), also summing to 6, symbolizing balance and harmony.

My Golden birthday was another moment of numerical alignment, occurring when my age matched my birth date exactly. At 24, the synchronicity again revealed layers of meaning: 2+4 equaled 6, paralleling my place as the sixth child. Even more striking, the year 1986 itself was numerically significant—1+9+8+6 summed neatly to 24, echoing the date of my birth.

These numerical synchronicities deepened dramatically on my diamond birthday in 2024. The day, Wednesday, mirrored the exact weekday of my birth, January 24, 1962. My age, 62, matched my birth year precisely. The year itself, 2024 (2+0+2+4), totaled 8, reflecting the number of children in my family. Furthermore, considering my life path number 7—a mystical and spiritual number—echoed poignantly as seven survivors remained in my family in 2024.

Even the weekday contributed numerologically: Wednesday, the third day of the week, combined with the date and my birth year (3+1+2+4+1+9+6+2) summed to 28. When simplified, 2+8 yielded 10, representing the complete family number when we were all present— two parents and eight children.

These numerical patterns reinforce my belief in the profound synchronicity woven through life's milestones. Birth charts have always been an inspiring guide in my journey, illuminating paths of self-discovery and spiritual insight. Let's explore together the deep significance and revelations your own birth chart may unveil, connecting you, too, to the intricate synchronicities of your personal story.

CHAPTER XXVII
Is there such a thing as an
Insignificant Synchronicity?

This chapter explores the deeply personal significance of synchronicity, numerology, and energetic resonance during times of transition. It demonstrates how aligning with symbolic numbers and messages from the universe can affirm our path and offer reassurance during moments of change.

While synchronicities can significantly influence our lives, it is crucial to understand that not all synchronicities bear the same immediate or obvious significance. At times, what we interpret as synchronicities may seem random or coincidental, prompting us to wonder if we should simply wait and observe their true meaning over time. Reflecting deeply on this, I have come to believe that all synchronicities, no matter their apparent magnitude, carry an intrinsic value.

Occasionally, we encounter synchronicities that may not drastically alter our life paths but nevertheless captivate our curiosity or evoke a sense of wonder. Minor synchronicities—like repeatedly noticing a specific number or unexpectedly hearing a meaningful song—might initially seem trivial, but they hold subtle reminders of life's underlying connectedness. These moments can gently nudge our awareness, inviting reflection and reinforcing the idea that our lives are interwoven with hidden patterns.

Conversely, profound synchronicities can dramatically reshape our trajectories. These impactful experiences typically coincide with pivotal moments, such as encountering a significant person who changes our life direction, receiving a timely and powerful message, or discovering a coincidence that grants transformative insights. These extraordinary moments resonate deeply, guiding us with clarity and purpose.

Learning to discern the varied significance of synchronicities can foster substantial personal growth. Not every synchronicity provides immediate clarity or profound revelations about ourselves and the universe. However, even the seemingly mundane ones carry potential, quietly preparing us for deeper awareness and understanding in future circumstances.

Every synchronicity, significant or subtle, holds implications that can enrich our lives by offering valuable perspectives, guidance, or moments of meaningful connection. These synchronicities, even if seemingly minor, remind us of the delicate threads that bind the fabric of existence, enhancing our appreciation of life's intricate tapestry.

Dr. Seuss, in his beloved children's story Horton Hears a Who, famously declared, "A person's a person, no matter how small." This profound yet simple truth extends beyond people, encompassing the events and signs that shape our lives. Just as every individual deserves recognition and acknowledgment regardless of size or perceived importance, every synchronicity, no matter how subtle, deserves our mindful attention.

Ultimately, no synchronicity is insignificant. Even those we initially overlook or dismiss can carry meaningful revelations. Embracing each synchronicity with openness and curiosity allows us to unlock their deeper messages, enriching our lives and strengthening our sense of connection to the universe.

A Couple of Unexpected Appearances

The unexpected appearance of an Egyptian-themed screensaver, particularly the Pyramid and the Sphinx, right after settling into my new home and starting up my computer. It was 9:30 a.m. The Pyramid represents strength, ancient wisdom, spiritual awakening, and the journey toward enlightenment. Similarly, the Sphinx symbolizes mystery, hidden knowledge, and timeless truths, serving as a guardian of sacred secrets. This unexpected digital appearance could signal that I was entering a profound phase of spiritual discovery and growth, inviting me to explore deeper truths hidden beneath life's surface.

Additionally, noticing the synchronicity at exactly 9:30 am is meaningful. The numerological breakdown ($9+3+0 = 12 \rightarrow 1+2 = 3$) strengthens this sense of divine orchestration. The number three resonates with profound spiritual significance:

The Divine Trinity

In numerous spiritual traditions, the number three symbolizes profound truths about unity within diversity. In Christianity, it represents the harmonious union of Father, Son, and Holy Spirit—distinct yet indivisible, reflecting the ultimate balance between the divine and human realms. Likewise, Hinduism recognizes the sacred triad of Brahma, Vishnu, and Shiva, embodying creation, preservation, and destruction. Both traditions remind us that divine power expresses itself through balanced interplay among complementary forces, teaching that true spirituality lies not in isolation but in harmonizing the different dimensions of our existence.

Creative Expression

Three carries with it the essence of creativity—an ever-flowing energy that encourages us to tap into the deep wells of inspiration within ourselves. When this energy moves through us, creativity becomes effortless, manifesting through photography, painting, writing, music, or any art form we feel drawn toward. In my own life, photography has become an inspired expression, a sacred way to connect with and honor divine presence. The creative act becomes an authentic reflection of our innermost selves, and in sharing these authentic expressions, we channel and reveal the divine essence within.

Communication and Collaboration

Spiritually, the number three resonates strongly with clear and meaningful communication. It symbolizes not only the act of speaking but also active listening and openness to dialogue. People influenced by the energy of three often find themselves naturally gifted in communication—articulating ideas with clarity, empathy, and effectiveness. The number also highlights the importance of collaboration, reminding us that true understanding often emerges from unity and cooperation. By communicating openly and working harmoniously with others, we can collectively manifest visions that surpass individual capacities.

Expansion and Growth

The vibration of three gently yet persistently encourages expansion beyond our comfort zones. It calls us toward growth, exploration, and continuous self-discovery. When we align ourselves with its expansive nature, we become receptive to abundant possibilities, new experiences, and spiritual evolution. The number three teaches that life is most fulfilling when embraced fully, without fear or hesitation. In opening ourselves to the vastness and beauty of existence, we invite meaningful opportunities for transformation and deeper self-awareness.

The Trinity Within

Perhaps most significantly, the number three calls our attention inward, toward the sacred trinity of mind, body, and spirit. Spiritual harmony is found when these elements are nurtured, respected, and balanced. Recognizing and tending to our internal trinity allows us to experience profound inner peace, wholeness, and fulfillment. Through intentional care for our mental clarity, physical wellness, and spiritual depth, we cultivate a holistic sense of self, rooted deeply in divine truth.

This framing creates a flowing narrative that seamlessly connects the various facets you've identified. Would you like to further expand or personalize any section to deepen its resonance with your own experiences?

During the height of the COVID-19 pandemic, my hypnotherapy practice temporarily closed, compelling me to take up a concierge position at SOBA condominiums located at 203 Catherine Street in Ottawa, Ontario. It was here, amid unexpected circumstances, that synchronicity revealed itself in beautifully subtle yet profound ways.
One memorable day, I spoke with Celeste Colpaart, a real estate representative at SOBA, about the significance of the number three. Our conversation danced around the mystical power this number holds, touching briefly on its symbolism before our exchange ended. Later that evening, as if the universe itself had been listening, Celeste sent me an image of her clock filled with combinations of the number three. This spontaneous gesture reaffirmed our interconnectedness and served as a

powerful reminder from the universe that we are indeed walking along our intended path.

Moments of synchronicity like these invite us to remain open, mindful, and receptive. However, the greatest challenge on this journey is cultivating a state of mindlessness—an open state free from ego, bias, or preconceived notions. Recognizing and overcoming the distortions of memory, whether tied to our immediate past, distant memories, or even previous lifetimes, is essential for true self-actualization.

Reflecting on numerology, I've discovered profound meanings embedded in numbers that consistently appear throughout my life.

The number three, for instance, symbolizes creativity, intuition, and balance. It represents life's fundamental triads: mind-body-spirit, past-present-future, birth-life-death. Many spiritual traditions honor this triune symbolism, seen clearly in the concept of the Father, Son, and Holy Spirit. Three ignites creativity and passion, bringing luck and success.

Number six, embodying harmony and balance, signifies compassion, intuition, and caregiving. Numerologically, it's recognized for its nurturing essence. Six uniquely stands out in mathematics as the first perfect number, its divisors (1, 2, and 3) summing perfectly to itself. Symbolically, it connects deeply with intuition—the sixth sense—and resonates fundamentally with organic life, as carbon holds an atomic number of six.

The number eight resonates with abundance and prosperity. Spiritually, it bridges the conscious and subconscious, blending the physical and spiritual realms. Its presence serves as a reminder that our present actions shape our future realities—we reap precisely what we sow.

Number nine holds the sacred space of fulfillment, wisdom, and spiritual enlightenment. It encourages self-reflection and aligns us with our higher purpose. Its mystical resonance is visible everywhere—from the 360 degrees of a circle (3+6+0=9) to the spiritual symbolism across diverse traditions: the nine fruits of the spirit in Christianity, Hinduism's nine universal elements, and the structured symbolism in the Temple of Heaven's architecture.

Nikola Tesla's fascination with the divine code—3, 6, and 9—further illuminates these numbers' profound roles as the keys to understanding the universe's mysteries. The sequence encapsulates creation's essence, echoed in natural forms through the golden ratio, underlying all existence.

Integrating these insights into daily life can be transformative. The 3-6-9 manifestation technique exemplifies this integration, harnessing the universe's energetic language by consciously aligning our intentions with cosmic vibrations. Writing down intentions three times in the morning, six times at noon, and nine times at night becomes an active dialogue with the universe, opening pathways to manifest desires authentically.

Through awareness of these synchronicities and numerical meanings, our journey unfolds with clarity and purpose, guiding us gently toward spiritual awakening and alignment with our true selves.

Numbers are far more than mere tools for counting; they are keys to understanding the deeper mysteries of existence. Throughout history, numbers have served as profound symbols in spiritual teachings, religions, mythologies, and philosophies across cultures. Ancient civilizations, from the Egyptians and Babylonians to the Mayans and Greeks, saw numbers as divine languages—cosmic codes holding the secrets to life's hidden order.

When you frequently encounter repetitive numbers like 1111, 1010, 333, or 999, you're not simply noticing random digits; you're tuning into a universal dialogue. Such synchronicities occur when your inner state resonates with external events, creating meaningful coincidences. These numerical patterns serve as messages, guideposts intended to illuminate your spiritual path, offer reassurance, or alert you to a needed shift in awareness.

Take, for example, the repetitive occurrence of the number 1010, connected deeply to my late friend Eddie Klotz. Eddie's rhythmic chant, "101033, 101033," became more than just an amusing personal quirk—

it was prophetic. After his passing on January 30 (notably represented by the number 10), the frequency with which I saw the number 1010 skyrocketed, manifesting in ways impossible to dismiss as mere coincidence. Eddie and I shared a profound connection to Egypt, the land of sacred mysteries. His initials, ECK, symbolically resonated with "Eckankar," or "co-worker with God," pointing toward a higher spiritual truth embedded in the fabric of our intertwined destinies.

These recurring numbers often arise during periods of profound spiritual awakening, when your consciousness shifts and expands, compelling you to question the deeper meaning behind seemingly mundane events. Numbers, in these phases, become spiritual breadcrumbs leading you toward heightened intuition, clarity, and self-awareness. Seeing the same numerical sequence repeatedly can feel uncanny, unsettling even. Yet this is precisely the moment when you are being called to pause, reflect, and acknowledge that a deeper truth seeks your attention.

My experience at SOBA condominiums vividly demonstrates this. As I conducted safety inspections, ascending and descending those steep stairwells, an inexplicable sense of familiarity overtook me. Despite having never physically been there before, every step felt like retracing an ancient path—echoes from another life, another time. This uncanny sensation linked me directly to the stairwells within the Great Pyramid of Egypt, an extraordinary synchronicity suggesting connections far beyond my immediate understanding. While skeptics might dismiss this parallel, those familiar with the intricate language of synchronicity understand the significance of such profound resonance.

To truly benefit from these numerical synchronicities, you must approach them mindfully, with an open heart and attentive mind. When repetitive numbers appear, pause briefly, offer gratitude, and reflect inwardly. Ask yourself, "What am I being guided toward?" This moment of reflection enhances your intuitive capacity and aligns you with the universe's subtle currents.

In essence, numbers are spiritual markers, guiding your soul through life's complexities. They remind you of your connection to something greater—an invisible thread binding all existence. By paying attention to these signals, you become an active participant in a universal dialogue, moving closer toward a profound understanding of who you are, why you are here, and how beautifully interconnected everything truly is.

Why This Matters

Recognizing meaningful patterns, especially during pivotal life shifts, nurtures trust in divine timing and encourages us to live more intentionally. Even subtle synchronicities serve as reminders of unseen support and guidance.

Have you ever noticed numbers or signs recurring in your life? What meaning did they hold for you? How might you become more aware of these signs and what they could be trying to tell you?

CHAPTER XXVIII
Remembering Forward

This chapter invites readers to explore the ancient and globally resonant concept of reincarnation—not as dogma, but as a philosophical lens through which to view the continuity of the soul. Through comparisons across faiths and personal insight, it suggests our lives may be part of a greater spiritual unfolding across time.

The captivating idea of reincarnation—the rebirth of the spirit into a new body—has intrigued humanity for thousands of years. Across cultures and epochs, it has posed timeless questions about life's purpose and the mysteries beyond our physical existence. Esteemed Greek philosophers like Pythagoras, Socrates, and Plato pondered this very phenomenon, believing that a soul's destiny was intricately tied to its actions in previous lives, laying a philosophical cornerstone for spiritual immortality.

While mainstream Christian and Islamic traditions generally reject reincarnation, subsets within these faiths—such as the Cathars, Alawites, Druze, and Rosicrucians—embrace it. These groups reflect beliefs echoing ancient Roman and Indian spiritual teachings, highlighting reincarnation's widespread and enduring influence across civilizations.

The ultimate spiritual aim across many traditions—moksha, nirvana, mukti, or kaivalya—is liberation from the relentless cycle of rebirth. However, Buddhist, Hindu, and Jain perspectives differ on critical points, including what precisely reincarnates, the mechanics behind rebirth, and the path toward spiritual freedom. In Buddhism, the doctrine of "anatta," or no-self, posits a transient consciousness rather than a permanent soul. Hinduism, conversely, emphasizes an eternal spirit, the atman, journeying through multiple incarnations toward liberation. Jainism, too, sees the spirit or Jiva as eternal, cycling through lives shaped by accumulated karma until ultimate liberation through ascetic discipline is achieved.

The origins of reincarnation beliefs remain mysterious, but ancient Indian civilizations—the tribes along the Ganges and Dravidian cultures in South India—are likely sources. The Vedic religions, dating back to around 1500 BC, laid early groundwork with karma and rebirth concepts. These beliefs were more deeply explored in the Upanishads around the 8th century BC and later elaborated through Buddhist, Jain, and various Hindu philosophical traditions.

The cyclical nature of reincarnation resonates profoundly with the Buddhist concept of saṃsāra—the continuous wheel of life, death, and rebirth, vividly depicted in the Bhavacakra or "wheel of existence." Each rebirth, determined by one's karma, underscores the interconnectedness of actions across lifetimes. Yet, liberation—nirvana—remains the ultimate goal, even though modern practitioners often focus on earning merit to ensure better subsequent lives.

Why This Matters

Considering reincarnation opens a deeper dialogue about the soul's journey, karma, and our interwoven destinies. It encourages compassion, introspection, and accountability for our actions while offering comfort that nothing meaningful is ever truly lost.

Have you ever experienced a moment of déjà vu or an inexplicable connection to a place or person? What might that moment be telling you about your soul's journey? If reincarnation were real, what lesson might you be carrying forward from another life?

CHAPTER XXIX
Echoes of the Soul:
The Compass of Synchronicity

In this chapter, we explore the mystical interplay between déjà vu, synchronicity, and past-life memory as echoes of the soul's deeper journey. Through personal stories and spiritual reflection, the narrative reveals how these uncanny moments are not coincidences, but signposts from a multidimensional self guiding us through lifetimes.

From fleeting sensations of familiarity to profound awakenings linked to ancient Egypt, the chapter invites readers to view life as a spiral of returning wisdom—where every moment may hold the key to a forgotten past and the compass for a higher purpose.

Some moments in life shimmer with a strange familiarity. A place, a person, a fleeting glance—we feel we've been here before, though reason tells us otherwise. These experiences, known as déjà vu, seem to open doors through time, beckoning us to remember something just beyond the veil.

This chapter explores the mysterious interweaving of déjà vu, synchronicity, and past-life memory—threads that, when followed, reveal the soul's subtle map. These are not just fleeting curiosities, but echoes of the eternal self, whispering through the noise of the present moment.

The Soul Remembers

Déjà vu, from the French "already seen," is more than a trick of the mind. It hints at the complexity of consciousness—possibly surfacing when present moments mirror past spiritual or karmic experiences. It feels like a nudge, a pulse of recognition from beyond time, guiding us to pay attention.

Carl Jung's concept of synchronicity, the experience of meaningful coincidence, reveals a similar mystery. These moments defy logic, suggesting an unseen harmony—a cosmic choreography. When synchronicity and déjà vu intersect, they often shake us awake, sparking questions about fate, purpose, and the hidden architecture of reality.

Perhaps they are not isolated phenomena at all, but two expressions of the same soul-language: a communication from our multidimensional self across lifetimes.

A Divine Intervention

In my own journey, synchronicity and déjà vu have appeared like spiritual breadcrumbs. One unforgettable moment took place in Waikiki, Hawaii. I encountered an elderly Asian woman, lost among the crowd. As I helped her find her hotel, I felt something beyond kindness—an unfolding.

After guiding her to safety, I lingered, gazing at the vast horizon. Then came a jarring epiphany: I had once lived as an Egyptian—someone prominent, but punished and erased from history, fated to wander endlessly. The weight of that memory was soul-deep.

Suddenly, the rootless wandering of my present life made sense. I had lived in over thirty cities by the age of forty, always moving, never settling. What once seemed like impulsivity now revealed itself as karmic echo—a nomad soul chasing a home it could not name.

Luke 4:23 haunted me: "A prophet is not accepted in his hometown." A scripture, a whisper, a truth. Belonging had always eluded me, but now I understood: I was searching not for a place, but for remembrance.

Egypt's Whisper

In 1999, Hawaii called again. Without reason, I moved to Waikiki. The pull was powerful, yet I soon returned to Canada, my decision driven more by practicality than passion. But in retrospect, that brief move was another synchronistic flicker—a spark from a fire that burned in another life.

In 2001, I was staying with my friend Colin in Vancouver, feeling unmoored and unsure. Then I found a job posting that felt impossibly aligned: General Manager for The Blue Man Group at the Luxor Hotel in Las Vegas. I had the background. I had history in Vegas. It was uncanny.

I applied—and was immediately flown down. The hospitality was surreal. I met the performers, the managers, dined like royalty. One night, during a show, they spotlighted me in the audience. I stood, illuminated, addressed by the Blue Men themselves. I don't remember their words—but the energy of that moment branded itself into my soul.

And then... nothing. No call. No rejection. Just silence.

I now believe Egypt was calling—not to offer me a job, but to reawaken something dormant. The Luxor Hotel, built as a pyramid, with a beam of light shooting into the sky, symbolically echoed my ancient past. Egypt was speaking to me through modern mirrors.

Seeing Through the Lens of Spirit

During my early spiritual awakening, photography became my gateway. With every shot, I felt I was documenting the divine. Structures, sky, water—each image captured not just form, but essence.

One day in 2009, wandering downtown Los Angeles, I spotted a building bathed in blinding sunlight. Its rooftop shimmered like a beacon. I raised my camera. Click.

It felt like more than architecture. It felt symbolic. Like the Luxor's beam, this flare of light seemed to bridge time—modern concrete recalling ancient pyramids. I asked myself: Are we unconsciously building echoes of past sacred sites? Are our lives layered upon forgotten ones, trying to remember?

Egypt's whisper once again rose—soft but insistent.

The Ancient Within Us

Ancient Egypt continues to captivate us, not merely for its monuments, but for its mysticism. The pyramids, the hieroglyphs, the myths—they resonate with something old in us. They awaken ancestral knowledge about reincarnation, soul journeys, and cosmic purpose.

Perhaps we feel drawn to these ancient places not just as tourists, but as returning pilgrims.

Why This Matters

To recognize synchronicity and déjà vu as soul-messages is to awaken to a greater identity. We are not merely the sum of our current choices. We are echoes of lifetimes, voices layered across centuries, searching for integration.

Life is not linear—it is a spiral, revisiting key themes, offering us new ways to see and heal.

Think back to a moment when you experienced déjà vu—a fleeting sense that you had *been here before*, though logic said otherwise. What emotions did it stir in you? Was it comforting, unsettling, or deeply familiar in a way you couldn't explain?

Now consider: could this moment have been a message from your soul? A whisper from a past life or an inner knowing trying to guide your present path?

LUXOR HOTEL, Las Vegas, Nevada

CHAPTER XXXI
The Ka, The Corpus, and The Calling

This chapter bridges the wisdom of ancient Egypt and Hermetic traditions with the modern seeker's journey. Through beliefs in reincarnation, sacred rites, and esoteric teachings, it reveals a worldview where the soul evolves across lifetimes, guided by divine forces and universal truths encoded in both myth and memory.

The belief in reincarnation, or the cycle of rebirth, was central to ancient Egyptian spirituality. Egyptians saw the soul as immortal, composed of distinct elements—primarily the body, spirit, and the ka (life force). They believed that the soul traversed multiple lifetimes, experiencing numerous incarnations known as "ka incarnations," before achieving eternal peace in the Afterlife.

The Journey Through the Afterlife

The Afterlife was envisioned as a realm of judgment and purification. A soul's worthiness was determined by various trials, the most significant being the Weighing of the Heart ceremony. Here, the deceased's heart, symbolizing their moral essence, was weighed against the feather of Ma'at (truth and justice). Only those with hearts as light as a feather gained entry to eternal paradise.

The Significance of the Ka

Central to Egyptian metaphysics was the ka, viewed as the individual's life force and unique spiritual essence. Egyptians believed that one's earthly actions shaped the destiny of their ka in future incarnations. Complex rituals and elaborate funerary customs, including meticulous mummification practices and offerings, were intended to sustain and nourish the ka, thereby guiding it favorably into subsequent existences.

Memories of Past Lives

Ancient Egyptians perceived past life memories as accessible through dreams, visions, and spiritual revelations. Such experiences were often recorded and artistically depicted, offering glimpses into the soul's previous journeys. Stories embedded in mythology, rituals, and literature provided a cultural framework for comprehending these mystical past life connections.

Egyptian beliefs in reincarnation provided both spiritual context and existential hope, linking moral behavior with eternal continuity. The intrigue of this timeless tradition continues to captivate modern imaginations, bridging ancient wisdom with contemporary fascination.

Hermeticism: The Sacred Wisdom of Hermes Trismegistus

Hermeticism embodies an ancient tradition merging Greek and Egyptian mysticism through the figures of Hermes and Thoth. Thoth, the revered Egyptian deity of wisdom, writing, mathematics, and magic, known as Djehuty, or "He who is like the Ibis," was symbolically represented by an ibis bird or baboon. Hermes Trismegistus, a syncretic amalgamation of Thoth and Hermes, symbolizes the transmission of divine wisdom.

Hermetic Teachings and the Corpus Hermeticum

The teachings attributed to Hermes Trismegistus were compiled in sacred texts collectively known as the Hermetica. Among these, the Corpus Hermeticum, comprising seventeen Greek treatises dating approximately from 100 to 300 AD, remains the most influential. These writings span topics such as cosmology, spirituality, alchemy, and ethics, considered foundational for mystical wisdom.

Prisca Theologia and Hermetic Influence

Hermeticism profoundly impacted Renaissance philosophy through the theory of prisca theologia—the belief in a singular, original divine theology imparted by God to humanity. Scholars argued that Hermetic texts, alongside teachings from Zoroaster, Orpheus, Plato, Pythagoras, and Chaldean wisdom, preserved fragments of this primordial revelation. Early Christian theologians even associated Hermes Trismegistus with biblical figures such as Moses, Enoch, and Noah, reinforcing the belief in a divine origin of Hermetic knowledge.

Nag Hammadi Discoveries

In 1945, the discovery of Hermetic manuscripts near Nag Hammadi, Egypt, unearthed previously unknown dialogues, notably between Hermes and Asclepius, as well as "On the Ogdoad and Ennead," detailing Hermetic mystery schools. These texts, written in the Coptic language—Egypt's last ancient tongue—provide crucial insights into secretive teachings once guarded by initiates.

The Hermetic Brotherhood

In Alexandria, a clandestine society known as "the brethren" preserved Hermetic teachings through rituals such as spiritual baptism, sacred communal meals, symbolic greetings, and the study of esoteric texts. These practices echoed spiritual devotion and a pursuit of enlightenment, laying foundations influencing subsequent mystical traditions.

For further exploration into Hermeticism and related spiritual concepts, readers are encouraged to reference earlier chapters including "Alchemy: A Metaphysical Metaphor" and "Conscious-Centered Living: Calling Everything into Question," detailed extensively in prior editions.

Why This Matters

Understanding the Egyptian view of the ka, the afterlife, and past lives expands our spiritual vocabulary and deepens our appreciation for the continuity of the soul. Hermeticism further enriches this by showing how divine wisdom transcends cultures, inviting us to participate in an ancient yet ever-relevant pursuit of enlightenment.

What ancient wisdom or tradition do you feel mysteriously drawn to? Reflect on how the stories of reincarnation, judgment, or sacred teachings might mirror aspects of your own life journey. What might your "ka" be carrying from life to life?

CHAPTER XXXII
Premonition & Passage

This chapter explores the subtle and powerful realm of premonition—those mysterious moments when future truths are felt, seen, or known before they unfold. Whether through dreams, synchronicities, or unexpected images, these glimpses remind us that time is not linear and that deeper layers of consciousness constantly reveal guidance and meaning.

People have always been fascinated by the mysterious threads connecting past, present, and future—the inexplicable moments when intuition, dreams, or visions reveal hidden truths before they unfold. Throughout history, humankind has turned to fortune-tellers, oracles, prophets, and mystics, seeking guidance from those believed to possess precognition—the extraordinary ability to perceive future events. Films such as Premonition and Final Destination have explored these compelling themes, reflecting our enduring intrigue with the unknowable path ahead.

In my own life, premonitions arrived quietly, gently, often effortlessly—yet, occasionally, they brought profound, unsettling revelations. I never intentionally sought them out; instead, they chose me, manifesting through synchronicities, dreams, epiphanies, and gnosis. These mysterious experiences enriched my life immeasurably, opening doorways to spiritual growth and deeper understanding. However, among these moments, one premonition haunts me most vividly.

I've never hidden my deep longing to return home and reconnect with my family roots, despite knowing that such a reunion might never truly fulfill my desires. In 2017, compelled by an undeniable urge, I returned once again to my birthplace. It was there I discovered my oldest brother, Mike, gravely ill from a mysterious blood-related illness. True to our family's quiet stoicism—a legacy inherited from our mother—Mike silently bore his pain, never voicing complaints, even as his health rapidly deteriorated.

The heaviness surrounding his illness was intensified by the emotional turmoil our family faced. My sister-in-law, Margot, courageously cared not only for Mike but also for her aging mother and uncle amidst their declining health, amplifying the burden on their household. My primary concern turned immediately to my mother, whose emotional resilience had already been deeply tested by the loss of another son, John, only a few years prior. Mike held a special place in her heart, her favorite among eight children—an affection that, though unspoken, was felt deeply by all.

During the height of the COVID-19 pandemic, as Mike's journey on this earth neared its end, our family and friends visited informally, quietly, bidding farewell. I vividly recall entering Mike's room, seeing my niece, Jenny, beside his bed. Mike did not recognize my voice; he gently asked Jenny who had entered. "It's Uncle Chris," she softly replied. In that poignant moment, I absorbed the quiet acceptance on Mike's face, sensing he was prepared for what awaited beyond. The room held an aura of profound love, sadness, and serenity, as though time itself had paused in reverence.

After sitting with him in contemplative silence, I reluctantly departed, haunted by his imminent absence. He passed away shortly thereafter, leaving a persistent ache in my heart.

Some time later, while sifting through old photographs, I came across an image from a happier visit when Mike had come to see me at my home in Florida. Curious, I zoomed into the photograph, trying to discern what was playing on the television in the background. A chill rippled through me as I glimpsed the unmistakable image on the screen: my brother's face, precisely as it appeared in his final moments—quiet, accepting, poised on the threshold between life and eternity.

Words fail to fully capture the profound astonishment, the eerie realization that surged through me. Was this a glimpse of the future, a premonition subtly woven into an ordinary moment? How many other silent visions have passed unnoticed in the background of our lives, waiting to reveal themselves when the moment becomes clear?

Why This Matters

Premonitions challenge our assumptions about reality and the limits of perception. They connect us to something greater than ourselves, urging us to pay closer attention to the signs woven through daily life. This chapter honors the emotional complexity of these moments—especially when they involve those we love—and shows how spiritual insight can emerge even from loss.

Have you ever had a moment of déjà vu or a dream that later came true? Reflect on a time when you sensed something before it happened. What emotions did it bring up? What might this experience be trying to teach you about trust, time, and the mystery of life?

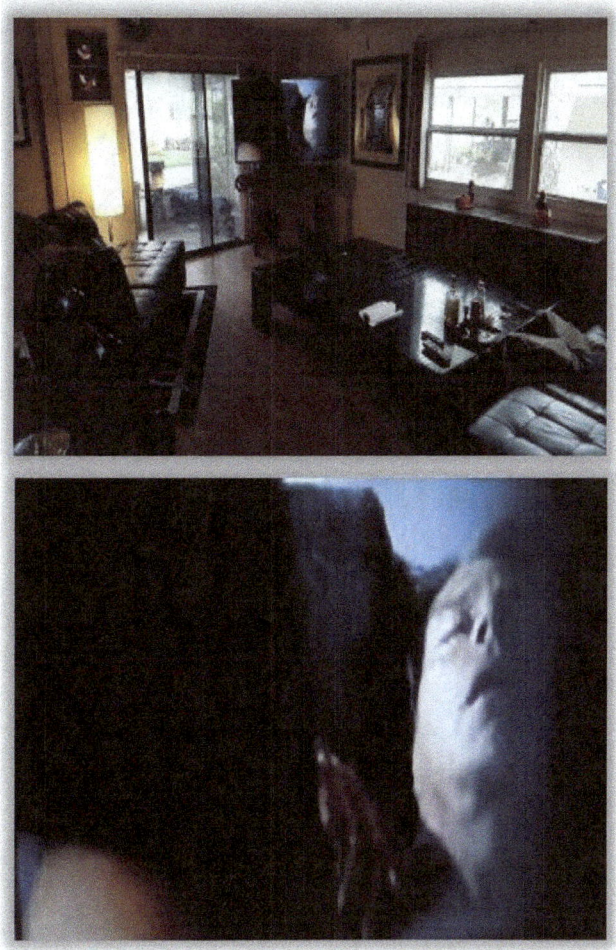

CHAPTER XXXIII
When Premonitions Speak

This chapter follows a cross-country road trip that unfolds into a profound journey of spiritual insight, intuitive guidance, and deep empathy. Through uncanny premonitions and energy impressions, the I experience the burdens of others' trauma, reinforcing the mysterious connection between soul-level sensitivity and emotional truth.

In 2014, I found myself experiencing an uncanny dance between premonition and reality—a strange precognition that blurred the edges of my world. The journey began rather ordinarily: a hopeful drive to Belleville to support my brother Mike's campaign for city council. The energy was palpable, charged with possibility, and by election night, victory was ours. Mike had won, yet the road beckoned me onward with its seductive promise of solitude, reflection, and adventure.

Impulsively, I embarked on a cross-Canada road trip, a journey mapped by intuition more than practicality. First, I planned to reconnect with Barb Mansbridge, an old friend living in High River, Alberta, then onward, tracing the coast down to Santa Cruz to visit David and Lee. Finally, my route would carry me back to the familiar warmth of Palm Springs. It was a path intertwined with friendship, memory, and an unconscious expectation of clarity.

Arriving in High River, a chill seeped into my bones as I pulled up to Barb's address. My heart faltered, pulse quickening, confronted by an empty lot—a void where a home once stood. Doubt surged briefly, forcing me to double-check the address, yet instinctively I knew no mistake had been made. I stared into the emptiness, my mind struggling to rewrite a truth it had already embraced.

After a disoriented pause, I approached a woman gardening nearby, seeking clarity. Her voice trembled slightly, recounting the devastating 2013 flood that had erased countless homes, including Barb's. Despite this logical explanation, my mind wrestled stubbornly against the brutal truth, haunted by the unanswered question: Where was Barb now?

The shadow of uncertainty lingered as I journeyed onward, eventually reaching San Jose and the secluded mountain home of David and Lee. The climb to their house filled me with an inexplicable dread—a foreboding sensation of descending into a darkness unseen. The landscape felt twisted, inverted; despite ascending upward, a suffocating downward pull enveloped me.

Yet, upon arrival, the warmth of David and Lee's welcome temporarily dispelled the unease. Their home, decorated tastefully and filled with art, felt comforting at first. We shared drinks, laughter, and stories infused with our shared Canadian roots, and eventually, fatigue guided me to my guest room.

Settling onto the bed, a disturbing wave overtook my thoughts. Without warning, invasive and alien feelings arose—haunting, disturbing notions of incestuous abuse involving my father, a torment I had never previously entertained. I lay paralyzed, confronting dark questions whose origins were elusive, foreign, yet painfully real.

Sleep eventually arrived, mercifully dulling the sharp edges of my confusion. By morning, sunlight offered gentle clarity, yet the troubling doubts still lingered, shifting uneasily within my mind. Descending the staircase into the bright kitchen, I found David already sipping coffee on the back patio, his laughter ringing bright and true.

After a few moments of casual conversation, the atmosphere shifted dramatically. David began sharing his own childhood traumas—mental, emotional, and shockingly, sexual abuse inflicted by his father. His openness stunned me into silent empathy, a profound revelation clarifying the disturbing energies I had unknowingly absorbed the night before. It became startlingly evident that my troubling premonitions had been a manifestation of David's hidden suffering, energy woven deeply into the fabric of his home.

Listening to David share his harrowing experiences, I felt privileged and humbled by his courage. He had chosen to speak to me, perhaps sensing my willingness to hold space for such profound vulnerability. My prior night's torment now held meaning, anchored in empathy rather than fear.

David's revelation brought me clarity, understanding the roots of his lifelong aversion to returning to his birthplace.

The remainder of the visit was quietly tender, the bond between us strengthened by the weight of shared truths. Although we never revisited that conversation, its impact lingered deeply within my soul, reinforcing the profound interconnectedness of human experience.

Years later, during a recent call with David and Lee, I learned of their ongoing struggles—Lee recovering from open-heart surgery, David confined by COPD yet still buoyed by his irrepressible spirit and laughter. In their resilience, I saw the reflection of our shared journey, each experience reinforcing the delicate, mysterious threads of empathy and precognition woven throughout life.

Reflecting now on that remarkable road trip, I'm left with the profound understanding that sometimes, life whispers its truths through subtle and mysterious ways—guiding us gently toward deeper compassion, empathy, and self-awareness.

Why This Matters

This chapter illustrates how energy and intuition can precede understanding. It shows how premonitions, even disturbing ones, may actually be messages from the collective unconscious or reflections of others' unspoken stories. These moments invite us to trust our empathic abilities and to approach others with compassion, not judgment.

Have you ever walked into a space and felt an emotional weight you couldn't explain? Reflect on a time when your body or spirit seemed to 'know' something before your mind could make sense of it. What did that experience reveal about your inner sensitivity—and how might you honor that gift?

CHAPTER XXXIV
All Roads Lead to Egypt

This chapter explores the mystical connections between neurological sensitivity (such as Asperger's), Egyptian symbolism, and life's subtle spiritual echoes. Through personal revelations, symbols like the asp snake and synchronicities surrounding ancient artifacts and friends' life paths, the narrative weaves a tapestry of past lives, intuitive gifts, and profound empathy.

Asperger's syndrome is often a subtle tapestry of invisible threads weaving through a life, shaping perceptions, interactions, and experiences in intricate patterns. At times, these threads become vividly apparent, especially for individuals known affectionately as Aspies, whose brains instinctively discern patterns—particularly in numbers, behaviors, and symbols.

In my journey, the discovery of Asperger's felt more like an acknowledgment of something known yet unnamed, a constellation emerging from scattered stars of misunderstanding and confusion. Years ago, a fleeting encounter with an individual whose name has faded from memory casually mentioned Asperger's syndrome, offering coping techniques. At the time, I dismissed it lightly; youth carried confidence in my uniqueness, not sensing the shadows cast by my atypical interactions.

Yet, as the years unfolded, the shadows became clearer, more tangible. Workplace interactions turned inexplicably hostile; colleagues seethed with anger at words I could not recall uttering. Socially, laughter erupted around me at statements I unknowingly made—statements so shocking yet humorous they refused to be repeated. I was labeled odd, an irony not lost on me, as I too found others peculiar, yet had never thought to voice it aloud.

Seeking clarity, I turned to online assessments. Each test consistently indicated a high probability of Asperger's. An official diagnosis, however, carried a prohibitive price tag of $4,000, uncovered by insurance, leaving me navigating an uncertain truth without definitive validation.

During one such moment of online introspection, an extraordinary synchronicity emerged from the shadows: ASPergers, or "Aspies," bore an uncanny linguistic connection to "asp," the Egyptian snake. My brain illuminated at this revelation, feeling the ancient pulse of synchronicity ripple through the realization.

The word "asp" traces back to the ancient Greek "aspis," meaning viper. Historically, "aspis" referenced venomous snakes of the Nile region, notably the Egyptian cobra. In dynastic and Roman Egypt, the asp symbolized royalty, its venom deemed noble enough to execute only the most esteemed offenders, granting them a dignified passage to the afterlife.

Intriguingly, Greek mythology deepened this symbolic resonance. Perseus, soaring across Egypt with the severed head of Medusa, unintentionally gave birth to asps from droplets of her blood, cementing the creature's mystical significance.

Such symbolic threads weave continually through my life, whispering connections across time and space. In 2009 and 2011, during my stays in Palm Springs, California, synchronicities again converged in poignant moments. My friend Daryl James cared for his elderly neighbor, Faye Conrad, a woman near ninety whose family had abandoned her. Her affection for Daryl was evident, even endearing.

On one visit, Faye recounted a visitation from Jesus. My curiosity piqued, I eagerly inquired about the divine message. Eyes closed yet alert, she retorted sharply, "None of your business," a humorous yet profoundly bittersweet interaction as she soon passed away. Daryl compassionately handled her affairs, including selling her mobile home.

Amidst decisions on my future, another synchronicity materialized. One sunny afternoon at Daryl's doorstep stood a man resembling Raggedy Andy—disheveled, drunken, yet charmingly vibrant. This rugged cowboy figure purchased Faye's mobile home, unknowingly stepping into a narrative of significance in my life.

Each synchronicity carries subtle clues, hinting at deeper connections, patterns, and truths woven into the fabric of existence. Like the asp's silent, regal presence in ancient Egypt, the threads of my Asperger's experience quietly influence perceptions, encounters, and revelations—reminding me continually to remain open to life's hidden whispers.

Eddie

They called him Eddie. Throughout this book, I have often referenced Eddie, a man whose kindness and generosity profoundly shaped my journey. In many ways, Eddie became the father I had always longed for, embodying a presence of warmth and guidance that resonated deeply within my heart.

Eddie owned Faye's house in Palm Springs through an unusual yet cherished friendship with Daryl and David, whom I previously mentioned in my reflections on Santa Cruz. Despite owning this property, Eddie primarily resided in North Hollywood, leaving the Palm Springs house largely vacant.

Upon returning from Hawaii, life delivered a striking coincidence—or perhaps, synchronicity—that brought me to reside in Eddie's newly acquired mobile home located at 900 Oahu Lane in Palm Springs, California. The address itself was profoundly symbolic, resonating with my previous life in Honolulu, Oahu—a place of significant spiritual experiences, including the supernatural encounter detailed in the chapter "A Divine Intervention." The synchronicity of finding myself on a street bearing the name of the island I once called home was both poignant and inexplicable.

As Eddie and I grew closer, we discovered a shared fascination with Egypt and its ancient mysteries. He owned treasured Egyptian scarabs and Native American spirit idols—items that spoke of his reverence for spiritual symbolism. Following his passing, I placed these cherished tokens into his urn as he was laid to rest with full military honors at the Riverside National Cemetery.

I recall vividly a transformative moment on New Year's Eve of 2004, walking home through the quiet streets of Palm Springs. On the side of the mountain, illuminated subtly by moonlight, appeared the striking profile of a half-man, half-monkey face etched into the rock face. Captivated, I hastily took a photo, though it turned out blurred and indistinct due to my anxious attempts to capture its magnificence.

Nearly two decades later, as I sifted through images of Egypt's sphinx and pyramids, a revelation struck me profoundly: the mysterious face I had glimpsed on that mountain years ago matched exactly a rarely highlighted detail of the Egyptian sphinx. This serendipitous connection reinforced my growing awareness of life's intricate patterns and the deeper interconnectedness threading through seemingly unrelated events.

All Roads Lead to Egypt

My residence at 8642 Franklin Avenue in Los Angeles was another setting for mystical encounters, notably the symbolic visions and revelations that appeared upon my shower wall. These homes in the Hollywood Hills, deceptively modest from the street, are carved spectacularly into the mountainside, concealing extraordinary interiors. High above this home at 1600 Mountcrest Avenue stood a distinctly pyramid-shaped house, a significance I only began to appreciate much later, after an incidental meeting with its owners.

The ancient Egyptian symbolism embedded within Tutankhamun's diadem—the unity represented by the cobra and vulture—mirrors the dual hemispheres of the human brain, symbolizing the harmonious blending of discernment and assimilation, intellect and spirit. Curiously, I had unknowingly collected symbols tied to this profound Egyptian iconography, including a soapstone carving of a vulture bought impulsively in Palm Springs in 2014. Though repeatedly tempted to part with it, an instinctual pull always compelled me to retain it, only recently revealing its profound symbolic value.

My journey toward deeper understanding took another synchronistic turn with the book Serpent in the Sky by John Anthony West. In 2021, driven by personal and familial considerations, I relocated to Ottawa, Canada, choosing proximity to my mother over other possibilities like Toronto or Montreal. My seemingly random decision to rent a modest basement apartment led me directly to Phred, the superintendent whose suggestion profoundly influenced my path. Phred insisted that West's book was revolutionary, challenging established dogmas surrounding ancient Egypt, a perfect addition to my ongoing doctoral research in conscious-centered living.

As I integrated Serpent in the Sky into my studies, synchronicities continued to manifest. On a routine check of my website traffic, I discovered an unexpected visitor from Chennai, India—the precise location where this influential book had been printed. This revelation affirmed my belief that nothing occurs by mere coincidence.

Years later, while casually exploring YouTube, a suggested video sparked my curiosity, reigniting memories of that profound New Year's Eve in Palm Springs, the half-man, half-monkey visage, and the eerie glowing figures reminiscent of Easter Island's Moai statues. Their resemblance, alongside connections to Egyptian pyramids and their celestial alignments, stirred questions I continue to explore. While the significance of the Moai in my personal story remains elusive, I sense clarity approaching, potentially unfolding as I complete the edition of Reading Life Backward 2025: Connecting the . . . Sacred Secretion, Synchronicity, Reincarnation, Hermeticism & Gnosis.

Why This Matters

Recognizing how neurological traits like Asperger's intersect with heightened pattern recognition and spiritual sensitivity opens the door to greater self-acceptance and understanding. By honoring both scientific and symbolic truths, the chapter affirms that our differences often carry spiritual gifts.

Have you ever experienced synchronicities that felt too meaningful to ignore? Reflect on a time when symbols, places, or numbers seemed to speak directly to you. What messages might they be offering about your path, your past, or your hidden gifts?

I wonder if the house was overlooking me or "looking over" me.

This chapter recounts a stormy drive from Los Angeles to Palm Springs that unexpectedly becomes a moment of synchronicity and spiritual reflection. The sudden emergence of the song "Kumbaya" and the subsequent news of Nelson Mandela's passing transform an ordinary commute into a sacred encounter with memory, music, and mortality.

I find myself reflecting on several compelling synchronicities that have recently surfaced in my life. Although these moments have yet to reveal their full significance or connection, I remain confident that their meanings will eventually become clear.

When the Sky Wept

On a particularly stormy day, I drove from Los Angeles toward Palm Springs, encountering relentless rain and dense traffic through the downtown corridor. Each raindrop seemed luminous, infused with a fragment of captured sunlight, falling heavily in a mesmerizing slow-motion dance. The windshield wipers strained against the torrent, amplifying a feeling of surreal isolation amid the congestion.

Suddenly, an unsettling sense of dread washed over me, accompanied by the unexpected and haunting melody of "Kumbaya," pulling forth memories of someone I hadn't thought about in years. Despite my unease, I eventually arrived home safely. The following day brought news of Nelson Mandela's passing. Whether it occurred on the day of his death or during his funeral, the familiar tune of "Kumbaya" playing in the background created a poignant, mysterious resonance with the moment in traffic, deepening my sense of synchronicity.

Why This Matters

Sometimes the universe speaks in whispers—a song on the radio, a memory unearthed, a feeling of dread that foreshadows greater truth. These subtle signs connect us to the unseen, reminding us that moments of alignment between the inner and outer worlds can be profoundly meaningful. They urge us to slow down, reflect, and listen.

Have you ever experienced a song, scent, or sudden thought that seemed to carry a message or foreshadow something greater? Reflect on a moment when a seemingly ordinary experience revealed a deeper emotional or spiritual layer. What did it awaken in you?

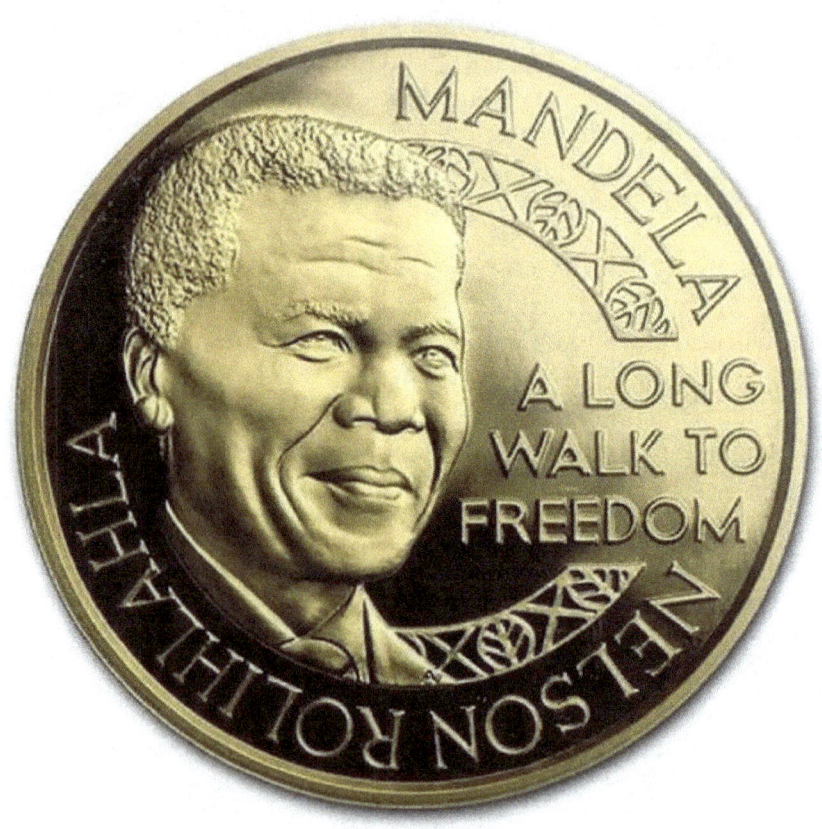

CHAPTER XXXVI
What We Try to Erase

This chapter explores the personal and symbolic meaning behind tattoos—how a youthful decision driven by inspiration can later become a marker of synchronicity, spiritual evolution, and even poignant loss. The narrative intertwines celebrity, memory, and mortality in an unexpected encounter that circles back on itself.

In the mid-1980s, as a young adult living in West Hollywood, California—a dramatic contrast from my upbringing in the tiny village of Corbyville—I became intrigued by the tattoo trend sweeping through the city. Though not one to typically follow trends, the idea of a subtle tattoo appealed to me. On Christmas Day, while strolling with friends down Sunset Boulevard, we discovered an inviting tattoo parlor. After thoughtful consideration, I settled on the lambda symbol, the eleventh letter of the Greek alphabet, valued numerically at thirty and symbolic of freedom and liberty.

Interestingly, my inspiration was Lorenzo Lamas, the charismatic star of the television series Falcon Crest, whose tattoos I had admired. Decades later, in 2006, I returned to Beverly Hills as a business manager for entertainment industry figures, including the renowned celebrity plastic surgeon Dr. Frank Ryan. Frank was known not only for his high-profile cosmetic procedures but also for charitable tattoo removals, especially for former gang members seeking new beginnings. I myself began the process of tattoo removal at Frank's clinic, though circumstances prevented its completion.

In a poignant twist, Lorenzo Lamas himself entered the clinic one day seeking tattoo removal. Amused by the synchronicity, I shared with him how he had inspired my own tattoo journey. The irony of our parallel paths, converging decades apart in the same Beverly Hills office, was striking.

Dr. Ryan tragically passed away in 2010, in a fatal car accident along the Pacific Coast Highway. Minutes before his accident, he had posted a serene photograph of his border collie, Jill, atop a Malibu dune—a haunting prelude to the tragic event. I had repeatedly warned Frank about his dangerous habit of texting while driving, particularly on those perilous Malibu roads—a warning that, sadly, proved prophetic.

Why This Matters

Tattoos often carry personal stories and cultural meaning. This chapter shows how our bodies can become living canvases of transformation—how what we mark externally can symbolize internal journeys. It also highlights the mystery of coincidence and the delicate power of warning, especially in the face of tragic endings.

Do you have a tattoo—or have you ever wanted one? Reflect on what symbol you would choose to represent your journey. What does your body remember that your mind might have forgotten? What stories live in your skin?

CHAPTER XXXVII
The Art That Found Me Again

This chapter captures two powerful synchronicities connecting art, time, and memory—from a Montreal-acquired painting echoing in an episode of Star Trek, to a Michelangelo sketch from the Sistine Chapel appearing in the background of a 1960s sitcom. These moments remind us how symbols transcend space and time, quietly anchoring us in a web of mysterious connection.

While living in Montreal in 2004, I acquired a captivating yet enigmatic piece of artwork depicting a figure, possibly of Asian descent, tenderly holding a child. Its gender ambiguity and gentle embrace resonated deeply, symbolizing universal love and acceptance. Before departing Montreal, I entrusted this piece to my neighbor and artist friend Steve Andrew.

Years later, I noticed an uncanny resemblance while watching an old episode of the original Star Trek series titled "Assignment: Earth." The same—or astonishingly similar—artwork hung in the background of a scene. Given the geographic and temporal improbabilities, this synchronicity felt profound and inexplicable, leaving me marveling at the mysterious connections woven through life.

Michaelangelo and "That Girl" - Tilted Frame, Perfect Timing

In 2021, working remotely from Ottawa, I often had the 1960s sitcom That Girl playing quietly in the background. During a brief pause, I noticed a familiar image on the wall of the set—Michelangelo's Study of a Head, a preparatory sketch for his Sistine Chapel frescoes. Astonishingly, I owned the same print, displayed in an aged metal frame with cracked glass, its print slightly askew. Although it may not have been the identical object, the probability of such a coincidence felt remarkably slim, further deepening my intrigue with the invisible threads linking seemingly unrelated experiences.

Why This Matters

The presence of meaningful images in unexpected places suggests that nothing is truly random. Whether through art, dreams, or media, the soul recognizes what the mind may overlook. These echoes affirm that our journey is not isolated but threaded with deeper truths—if we have the eyes to see them.

Have you ever come across an image, object, or phrase that stopped you in your tracks? Reflect on a time when something familiar showed up in an unexpected way. What memory did it stir? What deeper connection might it be pointing you toward?

CHAPTER XXXVIII
Urban Glyphs

This chapter reflects on the quiet power of everyday synchronicities, showing how subtle intersections—like business names, familiar street corners, or number patterns—can serve as gentle nudges from the universe. These signs remind us to pay attention, as even the smallest clues often carry profound meaning.

Finally, I observed a quiet yet meaningful synchronicity on a street corner in Ottawa, at the intersection of Metcalfe and Nepean Streets. Two establishments stood diagonally from one another: Pico Pizza and Indigo Parking. Both names carried deep significance in my life. Pico reminded me of Bob Morelli's Pico Union Pawn Shop in Los Angeles, closely tied to my initial spiritual awakening at 8642 Franklin Avenue. Indigo connected to my profound spiritual experience in Honolulu, where I worked as a comptroller at the celebrated restaurant Indigo, marking a pivotal chapter of divine intervention in my life.

These subtle connections, though seemingly small or random at first glance, reinforce my belief that every synchronicity, no matter how seemingly minor, is part of a grander narrative yet to fully unfold.

REMEMBER:A synchronicity is a synchronicity, no matter how small.

Being aware of changes before they impact your daily life offers tremendous advantages. It allows you to adjust proactively instead of ignoring signals until life feels chaotic. Embracing these shifts in feelings and thoughts as they emerge leads to a smoother, more rewarding experience of heightened awareness.

Why This Matters

By staying attuned to life's symbolic language, we sharpen our awareness and cultivate spiritual presence. Recognizing these patterns fosters inner alignment and affirms that we are never truly lost—only gently redirected by forces greater than ourselves.

What small signs have shown up in your daily life lately—names, numbers, places? Reflect on a moment when something minor sparked a strong emotional or intuitive reaction. What might it be trying to tell you?

CHAPTER XXXIX
Physical, Emotional & Spiritual Markers of Awakening

From my firsthand experience, here are some important examples:

Headaches and Migraines: Feeling fuzzy-headed may signify your brain forming new neural pathways, creating fresh thought patterns. Embracing these changes without resistance makes the transition easier. Stay hydrated and rest, especially during major cosmic events.

Spiritual Flu: This energetic flu resembles physical flu symptoms but typically lasts only 24 hours. During this period, a spiritual fire rises within, purifying and elevating your cells to higher vibrations.

Feeling Unseen: As your energy rises, you might find others overlooking you or even bumping into you. Rather than feeling discouraged, recognize this as evidence of your changing vibrational frequency, creating temporary disconnection from others.

High-Vibration Sounds: Hearing a tuning-fork-like resonance in your ears signals your energetic body absorbing high-frequency information. Consider these sounds as instructions for your spiritual growth. Acknowledge them with gratitude, allowing clarity and awareness to follow.

Dizziness: Cosmic events like solar flares and eclipses can cause dizziness. Ground yourself by connecting physically with Earth—consider grounding products from Earthing.com, mentioning "Reading Life Backward."

Thymus Fluttering: Heart palpitations or fluttering sensations over your sternum indicate the thymus gland (your spiritual awakening gland) activating. Tapping gently on your sternum helps ground you during these expansions.

Tears and Emotional Release: Increased emotional sensitivity and tears reflect your heart field expanding, enhancing empathic abilities.

Tears symbolize cleansing old energy. Grounding yourself barefoot in nature helps manage overwhelming feelings.

Shortness of Breath: Expanding heart energy fields may cause temporary breathing difficulties. Deep diaphragmatic breathing helps stabilize and regulate your energy.

Sleep Disruptions: Difficulty sleeping is common during significant transitions. Introduce meditation or spiritual reading at bedtime for better relaxation and rejuvenation.

Waking at 3:00 AM: Awakening at this time is when your soul is actively communicating. Engage in meditation or journaling to capture intuitive messages, prophetic dreams, or out-of-body experiences.

Physical Care: Prioritize high-vibrational nourishment through fresh, plant-based foods and hydration. Daily movement prevents energetic stagnation, particularly important during cosmic energy shifts.

Sore Muscles and Joints: Discomfort indicates the release of old, toxic energy from cells. Regular physical activity aids assimilation of higher vibrations, alleviating pain.

Wings of Light: Sensations between your shoulder blades signify developing spiritual energy fields metaphorically called wings of light. Tightness or heaviness transitions into feelings of lightness as spiritual growth continues.

Clumsiness: Dropping objects frequently indicates old methods no longer serve you. Adjust your approach by staying present and focused, avoiding unnecessary distractions.

Anxiety Management: Heightened sensitivity to energy fields, especially during intense cosmic shifts, can manifest as anxiety. Maintaining awareness of your energy field rather than absorbing others' can stabilize emotions.

Memory Loss: Increased present-moment awareness may cause temporary memory lapses. Embrace this as a shift toward living fully in the now, not as cognitive decline.

Yearning for Freedom: Physical manifestations may accompany deep desires to change life patterns. Take gradual, practical steps toward liberation, balancing boldness with thoughtful progress.

Relationship Changes: Spiritual growth can transform relationships. Some connections deepen, others dissolve. Approach these transitions with honesty, compassion, and openness to change.

Expectation Shifts: Awakening spiritually often heightens your personal standards. Recognize everyone's individual growth paths, cultivating patience and acceptance of yourself and others.

Finding Life Purpose: A deep yearning for purpose frequently arises, urging you toward authentic living. Listen closely to inner guidance prompting alignment with your true essence.

Dietary Changes: Reflecting on my own journey, adopting vegetarianism greatly supported my spiritual evolution, empathy, and compassion.

Questioning Teachings: Expanded consciousness might make previous teachings feel incomplete or misleading. Recognize this as an invitation to explore multidimensional realities, empowering personal accountability.

Energy Assimilation Periods: Periods of lower energy follow intense spiritual growth phases. Honor these moments as essential integration periods, following Hermetic principles of vibration and rhythm (Kybalion Principles 3 and 5).

Final Thought: Remember, your well-being is in your hands, especially during periods of profound spiritual transformation. Taking proactive care and staying aware facilitates smoother, more meaningful growth.

As this edition concludes, notice the bold numbers—3, 6, 9, 7, 8, and 10—reflecting their prominence in my birth charts and life. Consider what your numbers signify in your journey.

"YOU ARE THE RIVER!"

Remember and honor those who have impacted you profoundly. If they're living, reach out today!

CHAPTER XXXX
The Quiet Strength of Mothers
Memory of a Nine Year Old

In the rhythm of laundry and the hush of twilight, we often find the hidden strength of women whose stories are rarely told. Behind every chore was a gesture of love, behind every task, a shield of protection. For mothers like hers, solitude wasn't loneliness—it was survival. These quiet moments under the stars, with arms full of laundry and heart full of weight, were sacred. They were pauses in a life that asked for everything and offered little in return. In remembering her, we remember all the mothers who carried more than they ever spoke, and whose strength we still walk in today.

The Quiet Strength of Mothers

Hanging Hope in the Dark

Summers were long in the country heat,
Just as long and hard as the winters were deep.
But hard wore a different face in July—
Not frostbite and firewood, but sweat in the eye.

With eight little mouths and one distant man,
She lived without choice, but always with plan.
No room for the seasons to dance in her mind—
Only tiredness constant, relentless, unkind.

I was the sixth, not the first to be dressed,
When it came to the extras, we simply made do with less.
But like many before me, I never quite knew
How empty the pockets, how faded the shoe.

With no money to spend, she got clever instead,
Making chores into games, to ease the thoughts in her head.
The basement became our kingdom of play,
Where laundry and laughter passed the long day.

The washer would hum, the rollers would spin,
We'd hold hoses with pride, never seeing the thin
Line between helping and staying in sight—
She kept us close in the daytime light.

The boogieman lived behind the old furnace,
We knew he was real, we felt his disturbance.
But he never came near when Mama was there—
Even monsters, it seems, knew better than dare.

We'd leap through the piles like miniature fools,
Chasing each other, breaking invisible rules.
Then the wringer would call us, the sacred last stage,
Where fingers met fate, and machines showed their age.

Sometimes a shirt, sometimes a hand,
Caught in the rollers we didn't quite understand.
She'd stop the whole world to rescue our skin,

With kisses and hugs, and we'd try it again.

By nightfall the work would slowly unwind,
We'd eat toast and jam with peace on our mind.
Old black and white glow, just two channels in range,
The string on the dial never did feel strange.

But always, when bedtime began to descend,
She'd slip to the backyard, her ritual to tend.
Hands raw with soap, arms heavy with care,
She'd hang out the laundry alone in night air.

Was it solitude or sorrow she found in the dark?
A breath of herself, a soul's little spark?
Perhaps those shadows gave her a space
To dream for a moment, to vanish from place.

For before he returned with his bottle and gloom,
She stood with the linens, beneath the full moon.
Not just hanging the clothes, but shedding the weight—
Of children, of silence, of unspoken fate.

Why This Matters

By reflecting on childhood memories shaped by scarcity, we begin to understand the emotional imprints left behind by early familial roles and responsibilities. The story emphasizes how hardship can co-exist with joy, and how children, even in challenging environments, find meaning in participation, belonging, and imagination. It also honors the quiet heroism of those who carry the weight of the world silently— mothers who give more than they receive, and who sometimes find their only solitude in the dark, hanging clothes alone.

Think back to your earliest memories of family and responsibility. What roles did you play as a child? How did your environment— whether nurturing or neglectful—shape your sense of self? Were there small moments of joy hidden within the challenges?

1. The Restless Knowing (Ordinary World)

Subtle discontent, sensing something deeper beneath the surface.

Chapter alignment: The River Within

- Reflection on meaning, moments, and the "in-between."
- Your intuitive unrest becomes the soil for transformation.

Quote: "Some of life's most meaningful moments aren't grand or dramatic. They arrive quietly."

2. The First Disturbance (Call to Awaken)

A psychic break or glimpse of another reality.

Events:

- The 'false UFO sighting' in LA
- A projected message from the sky

Symbol: The sky split open

Archetype: The Herald

3. The Inner Hesitation (Refusal of the Call)

Disbelief, emotional avoidance, ego resistance.

- Doubting intuition
- Feeling too strange to belong

4. Crossing the Threshold

Point of no return: you accept the strangeness and decode life symbolically.

Symbol: The Threshold of Knowing

Quote: "Truth, after all, is a gift—sometimes wrapped in discomfort, but always divine."

5. Meeting the Mentors

Wise figures, ancestors, dreams, or mystical guides appear.

Mentors:

- Your grandmother
- The 90-year-old golfer
- The psychic
- Water signs

Archetypes: The Sage, Oracle, Inner Teacher

6. Tests, Signs, and Sacred Trials

Synchronicities multiply. Testing your surrender.

- Water visions, stigmata-like signs
- Trust vs. disbelief

7. Descent into the Subconscious (The Abyss)

The ego breaks down. Illness or isolation opens the inner world.

8. The Secret Illumination (Revelation / Apotheosis)

Direct download of divine truth.

- Sacred Secretion awakening
- Gnostic realization: 'I am the story.'

9. The Return Begins

You re-enter the world with new eyes.

- Begin teaching, guiding, writing

10. Mastery of the Two Worlds

Walking in paradox—spirit/flesh, alien/human, teacher/student.

Symbol: Ouroboros

11. The Gift of Memory

Realization: your remembrance is medicine for others.

- The memoir becomes the mirror

12. Full Circle / Synchronic Return

You were never lost. You were becoming.

Tie-in: The River Rambles On — echoing your grandmother's legacy.

Quote: "I am not the author of this book. I am the page."

Stage 1: The Restless Knowing

Theme: The Quiet Stirring

"Some of life's most meaningful moments aren't grand or dramatic. They arrive quietly."

Symbolic Image Prompt

Visual Concept: A single flickering light at the end of a long hallway—soft golden glow surrounded by darkness, representing the first whisper of awakening.

Message from the Soul

You feel it, don't you? A sense that there's more—but it hasn't fully formed yet. It's alignment waiting to happen. You're not lost—you're listening.

Activation Practice: The Candle of Consciousness

Materials: A candle and a mirror.

1. Light the candle and sit in stillness.
2. Gaze into the flame, then into the mirror.
3. Ask yourself: *What have I always known, but never spoken aloud?*

Guided Reflection

- When did you first feel the sense that "this life" wasn't all there is?

- What recurring thought or image has followed you across the years?

Gnostic Whisper

"The soul speaks in symbols long before it speaks in words."

Stage 2: The Call to Awaken

Theme: Cracks in the Known

"The world doesn't always whisper. Sometimes it breaks open."

Symbolic Image Prompt

Visual Concept: A night sky split by light, with a hidden symbol appearing in the crack.

Message from the Soul

Something breaks through. A dream, a sign, a strange event. It doesn't need to make sense—it needs to be felt. You are being called not to understand, but to notice.

Activation Practice: Call and Echo

1. In silence, sit with the memory of a moment that "called" you.
2. Write it down exactly as it felt.
3. Ask: *What did it awaken in me?*
4. Draw or sketch the symbol it left behind.

Guided Reflection

- What moment or encounter felt like a rupture in the ordinary?
- Did you follow it—or retreat?
- What was the first thing you questioned afterward?

Gnostic Whisper

"Revelation sometimes knocks and sometimes pierces.."

Stage 3: Refusal of the Call

Theme: The Pull of Safety

"To awaken is to unsettle the part of you that learned to survive by staying small."

Symbolic Image Prompt

Visual Concept: A cloaked figure turning away from a glowing doorway.

Message from the Soul

You heard it—but you weren't ready. Fear disguised as logic. Safety disguised as purpose. You didn't fail—you paused.

Activation Practice: Shadow Talk

1. Write a letter from your fear.
2. Let it say why it wanted you to stop.
3. Then respond with compassion from your wiser self.

Guided Reflection

- What have you walked away from that still calls to you?
- Where do you confuse comfort with peace?
- What fear still speaks in your own voice?

Gnostic Whisper

"The soul knows—but the self must consent."

Theme: Stepping Into the Unknown

"You don't need a map. You are the doorway."

Symbolic Image Prompt

Visual Concept: An open door floating in space, surrounded by stars and silence.

Message from the Soul

You said yes—perhaps silently. You stepped forward without proof. That is the initiation.

Activation Practice: Threshold Walk

1. Go outside and walk without destination.
2. At each turn, pause and ask: *What am I stepping into?*
3. Whisper your intention aloud.

Guided Reflection

- What did you leave behind when you crossed your last threshold?
- What changed after you said yes?
- What name would you give to the part of you that crossed?

Gnostic Whisper

"The unknown is not empty—it is pregnant with purpose."

Theme: Earthly Angels and Echoes

"Guidance doesn't always come from someone wiser—it comes from someone timely."

Symbolic Image Prompt

Visual Concept: An old traveler handing a glowing orb to a child beneath a tree.

Message from the Soul

Look again. The stranger who stopped you. The words that echoed. The ancestor in your dream. You were never alone.

Activation Practice: Soul Lineage Sketch

1. Draw a spiritual family tree—not of blood, but of soul mentors.
2. Write one sentence of wisdom you've received from each.

Guided Reflection

- Who changed your life with a single sentence?
- Which guides are still with you, even if unseen?
- What part of you is now becoming a mentor for others?

Gnostic Whisper

"Every teacher is a memory disguised as a meeting."

Theme: Fire That Reveals

"Every sign is a question: Will you follow me deeper?"

Symbolic Image Prompt

Visual Concept: A labyrinth of flames, with soft footsteps walking its path.

Message from the Soul

Synchronicity tests your courage. Not because it wants you to fail—but because it needs your full yes. Trials are truth dressed in mystery.

Activation Practice: Elemental Journal

1. Choose fire, water, earth, or air.
2. Write a moment where that element tested you.
3. What did it burn away—or awaken?

Guided Reflection

- Which life challenge was actually a sacred test?
- What have you endured that made you more luminous?
- What does "resilience" mean to your soul?

Gnostic Whisper

"The test is not to survive—it is to remember."

Theme: The Sacred Undoing

"Before the soul ascends, it dissolves."

Symbolic Image Prompt

Visual Concept: A figure submerged underwater, still and glowing faintly, surrounded by drifting memories.

Message from the Soul

This is the unraveling. Illness, silence, solitude—they are not punishments, but portals. You are not disappearing. You are being re-formed.

Activation Practice: Submersion Meditation

1. Lie down and imagine being held in water.
2. Let go of effort.
3. Ask: *What part of me is trying to die with grace?*

Guided Reflection

- What have you lost that deepened you?
- When were you most still—and most changed?
- Who are you beneath what the world sees?

Gnostic Whisper

"The wound is not a break—it is a baptism."

Theme: Direct Knowing

"You are not learning—you are remembering."

Symbolic Image Prompt

Visual Concept: A brilliant burst of light inside the outline of a human form.

Message from the Soul

Revelation doesn't arrive—it is uncovered. What glows inside you now has always been there. Truth comes not as information, but as resonance.

Activation Practice: Crown Flame Breath

1. Sit upright, eyes closed.
2. Imagine a light at your crown.
3. Inhale into it. Exhale through your heart.
4. Repeat until stillness becomes glow.

Guided Reflection

- What moment of insight changed your path forever?
- What truth feels older than this lifetime?
- What does it mean to know without proof?

Gnostic Whisper

"What you seek is coded in your remembering."

Theme: Integration

"You do not return the same. You return as the message."

Symbolic Image Prompt

Visual Concept: A figure walking out of mist, holding a lit lantern shaped like a heart.

Message from the Soul

The journey inward was never for you alone. You rise now—not to escape the world, but to re-enter it differently. Your presence is the offering.

Activation Practice: Illumined Walk

1. Light a small candle or carry a crystal.
2. Walk your neighborhood as if seeing it for the first time.
3. Notice what calls to you.

Guided Reflection

- How are you now different in the same world?
- What old space feels newly sacred?
- What gift are you meant to carry back?

Gnostic Whisper

"You are not the seeker now. You are the spark."

Theme: Walking in Paradox

"To be whole is to hold both light and shadow—and bless them."

Symbolic Image Prompt

Visual Concept: A figure standing at the center of a yin-yang symbol, arms open.

Message from the Soul

This is the return to balance. Not purity. Not perfection. Integration. You no longer reject any part of yourself. You walk as both teacher and student, divine and human.

Activation Practice: Mirror of Two Faces

1. Sit with two photos of yourself: one joyful, one in pain.
2. Place them side by side.
3. Whisper: *Both of you belong.*

Guided Reflection

- What part of you once felt unworthy of light?
- What wisdom did your shadow carry?
- What does wholeness mean for you now?

Gnostic Whisper

"Enlightenment is not escape—it is embrace."

Theme: Becoming the Message

"The most sacred thing you can offer... is your story."

Symbolic Image Prompt

Visual Concept: An open book with golden threads weaving into the stars.

Message from the Soul

You've returned with treasure. Your memories. Your transformations. These are not just yours—they are mirrors for others. To speak them is to heal the world.

Activation Practice: Story as Offering

1. Choose a story from your life that once brought shame.
2. Write it from the voice of the soul.
3. Read it aloud—once, with love.

Guided Reflection

- What part of your story wants to be shared?
- What pain has become a gift?
- Who needs the light you carry?

Gnostic Whisper

"Your truth is someone else's permission to live."

Theme: The Sacred Return

"You are not at the end. You are at the remembering."

Symbolic Image Prompt

Visual Concept: A spiral returning to its center, glowing with soft light.

Message from the Soul

Here you are. Not finished. Fulfilled. Not perfected. Present. You haven't arrived—you've awakened. Life isn't a line. It's a spiral. And you are now walking it with open eyes.

Activation Practice: The Circle Ritual

1. Draw a circle on a page.
2. In the center, write: *I remember.*
3. Around the edge, write symbols, words, or names that brought you here.
4. Fold it and carry it with you for a day.

Guided Reflection

- What has returned to you that you thought was lost?
- What do you now know about time, truth, and transformation?
- Who are you now, at the center of your spiral?

Gnostic Whisper

"The end is never the end. It is the soul remembering it was whole all along."

Reading Life Backward: The Works of Dr. Christopher Graham, PhD CCHT

A Journey Through Synchronicity, Spirituality & Self-Discovery

Featured Titles

Reading Life Backward: In the Beginning
An introspective look at life's origins and synchronicities, blending personal reflection with metaphysical insight.

Reading Life Backward 2024: Calling Everything into Question
Challenges conventional thinking and embraces uncertainty as a pathway to growth and discovery.

Reading Life Backward 2025: Connecting the Dots
Explores the deeper patterns in life using stories and spiritual frameworks.

Reading Life Backward Full Circle (2012–2025)
A decade-long journey of inner work, revealing the interconnectedness of experiences across time.

Synchronicities Searching For Me (In Living Colour)
A vibrant, abridged celebration of personal evolution and divine timing.

Transformative & Spiritual Wisdom

The Art of Transformation
Unlocking change through hypnosis, Hermetic philosophy, and metaphysical healing.

Guardrails of the Soul
Modern reflections on the Ten Commandments and Seven Deadly Sins as spiritual guidance.

WHO ART: A Journey Through The Lord's Prayer
A devotional unpacking the relevance and depth of one of the most well-known prayers.

Guides for Life & Self-Discovery

TOP 100 THINGS TEENAGERS (everyone) SHOULD KNOW
Motivational life lessons from self-care to emotional intelligence—for teens and adults alike.

Falling Down & Growing Up
A heartfelt reflection on failure, resilience, and finding purpose at any age.

GETTING IN SYNC ~ Destination Me
A practical and intuitive guide to recognizing synchronicities on the path of personal alignment.

Stories, Plays & Human Insight

PERFECT PEGGY: A Woman's Duty
A powerful narrative exploring womanhood, sacrifice, and inner strength.

Three Contemporary Plays
Theatrical explorations of identity, society, and digital life.

TALK TO ME, ROBOT: A Conversation with ChatGPT
A creative look at the evolving relationship between humans and AI—with humor, heart, and insight.

Available now

Author: Dr. Christopher Graham, PhD CCHT

Explore the full collection and begin your journey of reflection and transformation.

www.ingramcontent.com/pod-product-compliance
Lightning Source LLC
Chambersburg PA
CBHW071747120626

46550CB00002B/693